TO BE A TRANS MAN

of related interest

Trans Power
Own Your Gender
Juno Roche
ISBN 978 1 78775 019 7
eISBN 978 1 78775 020 3

Not Just a Tomboy
A Trans Masculine Memoir
Caspar J. Baldwin
ISBN 978 1 78592 463 7
eISBN 978 1 78450 845 6

Transitions
Our Stories of Being Trans
Jessica Kingsley Publishers
Forewords by Sabah Choudrey, Juno Roche and Meg-John Barker
ISBN 978 1 78775 851 3
eISBN 978 1 78775 852 0

The Trans Self-Care Workbook
A Coloring Book and Journal for Trans and Non-Binary People
Theo Lorenz
ISBN 978 1 78775 343 3
eISBN 978 1 78775 344 0

Top to Bottom
A Memoir and Personal Guide Through Phalloplasty
Finlay Games
ISBN 978 1 78775 587 1
eISBN 978 1 78775 588 8

To Be A Trans Man

Our Stories of Transition, Acceptance and Joy

Edited by
Ezra Woodger

Jessica Kingsley Publishers
London and Philadelphia

First published in Great Britain in 2023 by Jessica Kingsley Publishers
An imprint of Hodder & Stoughton Ltd
An Hachette Company

1

A CIP catalogue record for this title is available from the British
Library and the Library of Congress

ISBN 978 1 78775 960 2
eISBN 978 1 78775 961 9

Printed and bound in Great Britain by Clays Limited

Jessica Kingsley Publishers' policy is to use papers that are natural,
renewable and recyclable products and made from wood grown
in sustainable forests. The logging and manufacturing processes
are expected to conform to the environmental regulations
of the country of origin.

Jessica Kingsley Publishers
Carmelite House
50 Victoria Embankment
London EC4Y 0DZ

www.jkp.com

Contents

Acknowledgements

I'd like to thank everyone at Jessica Kingsley Publishers, but especially Andrew James for giving me the opportunity to share and uplift some incredible voices. Isabel Martin, for being so patient even when I should have been sending emails so, so much more promptly than I actually did. Juno Roche, Sabah Choudrey, Meg-John Barker, Yvy DeLuca and everyone involved in the decision-making process for the JKP Writing Prize – this likely wouldn't exist without the opportunities you have given me. Kasper, Ezra, Caspar, Leo, Colton, Fox, Charlie, Rico – you were the best interviewees a man could hope for, and I'm so grateful that you all took the time to share with me stories, advice and wisdom. To Michael Williams, who helped me figure out if it was entirely insane to write a book while finishing my final year at university – deciding yes, but to do it anyway. To the Pride Writing Discord Server, thank you for letting me ramble about nonfiction writing, and giving me the space to explore and experiment with my writing in a safe environment. To my family, who had to deal with my panicked messages asking them to be quiet during the mountain of Zoom interviews, thank you for your patience. To everyone who made writing a book during a global pandemic bearable: friends, online and otherwise. To the cohort on the UEA MA Biography and Creative Nonfiction course – you weren't in my life when the bulk of this was written, but what you've taught me about writing in just a few short months is enough to warrant a mention. To all the trans men and transmasculine people in my life, and those not in my life. This is for you, first and foremost. Thank you.

Introduction

Sometimes, I forget I'm trans. Not that I think I'm cis – I wouldn't especially want to be, even if it were possible – but I just find myself settling into my body, accustomed to its curves and muscles, the way I never relax my shoulders properly and am constantly biting my lip. I exist within my skin, organs, parts and the feelings they carry with them. In my own mind, I am just a normal dude. Regardless of what I look like or how I feel about parts of myself, this is just my existence. I have far more important things to think about than the vast complexities of my feelings and my identity – and besides, after more than two decades of living in here, I'm more than used to it. I have spent my years in this form and in this life, getting to know the endless possibilities for human existence with the utmost intimacy. This, to use the term again (for lack of a better one), is my normal.

It's as if I forget that there's something Different-with-a-capital-D about me; that there is some wide, stretching, eponymous 'Other' of which I am part. Some bodies are like this, and some bodies are like that.

And then I see my housemate, six-foot-something and almost as wide as two of me put together, fry up and consume four eggs for breakfast. And then I remember. Sheepishly squeezing past him and his basketball shorts with a bowl of Raisin Bran (soya milk) and a black coffee, I clear my throat and my voice drops instinctively, muscle memory overriding the fact that over a year on testosterone makes the action almost utterly unnecessary.

'All right, mate?'

The action is funny to me now and brings back memories of the elaborate series of performances that were my childhood to teen years. Things I can laugh at now, secure in myself, but genuinely seemed like life-or-death in the eyes of a very, very anxious child. I remember I would always make sure that whenever I drank tea, it was always the strongest brew out of everyone's – the darkest shade of brown, three drops of milk maximum. I don't really know what I thought that said about me. Does strong tea make a strong person? And, by extension, a man?

Before I even knew who I was – before terms like 'transgender' or 'LGBTQ+'[1] entered into my vocabulary – I was always intent on making sure everyone knew I was strong. For child me, that meant never showing any emotion whatsoever and really hating hugs. I remember the first time I let my middle school best friend hug me; it was very dramatic, as most things are when you're on the cusp of puberty. We were both sitting on my bed, legs dangling loosely just off the floor. My walls were a deep

---

1   LGBTQ+ stands for lesbian, gay, bisexual, transgender and queer or questioning. The 'plus' represents other sexual identities including pansexual, asexual and omnisexual. Sometimes it includes an 'I' and 'A' (LGBTQIA+) signifying intersex and ally or asexual, respectively. Those I interview use variations of this initialism based on the language they personally use.

purple, and she had been sitting a little way away from me so our shoulders wouldn't touch. I remember feeling so sad that I thought I would explode, and she had told me that usually when someone was feeling that way, she would offer them a hug, but in this case, she wouldn't. I had bit my lip and awkwardly asked her to try, avoiding eye contact. She asked me to repeat myself, and I did, quietly, mumbling the words into my hair.

The reason I was so upset is lost to me now, but I made her promise not to tell anyone about it. As if I had some kind of reputation to uphold. It had been an awkward embrace, side-on, with very little reciprocation on my part. I don't think it lasted more than a few seconds at most. And that had been it, for a good number of years. Physical affection was my dirty little secret, to be squirrelled away into dark, private moments.

I could spend this entire book retelling the ways I stumbled through my own entirely fabricated preconceptions of masculinity, but I don't think that would succeed in doing anything beyond embarrassing me. I look back at that time with a wince, miles away from the kind of sad, scared, angry little boy that took pride in never crying. Everyone cringes at who they were, but there is a special kind of heat that rises to my cheeks when I think about the barriers I put up to ward away anyone who would dare get too close. Not a child, but instead a lone, solitary figure, set apart from those around me by righteous self-control. It's a little sad, but mostly it's just silly. What made me, at age 13, think I was so important that I had to be a bastion of strength for my weak, innocent friends?

I do still love a strong brew, though.

Sitting where I am now, in a slightly grimy student house in a less-than-ideal part of the city, I think about him. Or, rather,

I think about me. It's difficult to consider us as the same person if I'm being honest. As trans people, we can spend a lot of time distancing ourselves from the people we were pre-coming out, and I find myself especially guilty of attempting to scrub the past of any trace of him/me, save for a selection of carefully cultivated images. The picture I paint is one of stereotypical transness, of a child who showed all the signs and then some. I was the kid who always insisted on being the groom when we played weddings at nursery, or the kid who lost it and refused to come out of the changing rooms when my parents took us swimming because something was horribly, horribly wrong with the way I looked in my swimming costume. I never liked makeup, or dresses, or the colour pink. *You have to take me seriously as a man*, I seem to shout. *Isn't it obvious?*

And yet, in my desperate attempts to legitimize myself to what appears to be nobody in particular, I cut and carved away at myself and my history. I suppose it was my way of feeling better about myself, at a time when I had no community or resources to let me know that there were other options. I don't blame younger me for the actions of a sad child, but it did further alienate me from my sense of identity. Discarding anything that didn't fit into the model of 'trans boy poster child' left me with broken pieces of binary masculinity, a rigid gender construct that existed in a vacuum without context or positive connotations to fill in the gaps. I knew that I didn't like being who I was, but all the things I thought I had to do to change it required acting in a very specific way, or it wouldn't count.

I put myself and my masculinity in a box and locked it up airtight and didn't even notice that it quickly became impossible to breathe.

I started testosterone (T) on 21 June 2019. I was first referred to my gender identity clinic (GIC) around 2015, but various letter misplacements had slowed my journey to an almost unbearable crawl. Years of my life had been spent waiting for this moment. I put the Sustanon box down on the nurse's desk and took a seat while she prepared it, bouncing my leg eagerly. I'd expected to be nervous; sometimes I get weird about needles, despite six tattoos and counting. But I wasn't. I had never felt more ready for anything in my life. She apologized when she stuck the needle in, and I remember laughing softly. 'Honey,' I almost said, 'this thing could be serrated and I'd still thank you.'

I genuinely and utterly believe that testosterone saved my life. My chest dysphoria is still difficult to deal with and makes spending extended amounts of time with people a little more complicated, but I have no doubt in my mind that I would have died if not for hormone replacement therapy (HRT). My entire life felt as if it had been an old television, the kind that was staggering towards undignified obsolescence but you were desperate to keep going. Sure, you'd give it a whack and it would stop flickering to static, but it would never work properly, never get the colour contrast quite right. My saturation was always a little too low, and I viewed the world with a slightly greyish hue. Now, I am a person. And for the first time in almost two decades, I need to work out what that means.

Now that I am (more or less) cis-passing, I've come to realize that most of my concepts of masculinity have been built around trying to convince the world that I am man enough to stake a claim to it. From middle school me proudly listing all the Beatles albums chronologically, to wearing a minimum of three pronoun badges at any one time in sixth form, I had always been intent on setting myself apart from my peers, regardless of whether I knew the reason. The 'not like other girls' rhetoric had revealed itself to be dysphoria without a name, but its identification hadn't nullified the effect. If the world was a competition, the judges? Everyone to ever exist. And it is only now that I'm realizing the experience has been exhausting. When we are defined by our opposition to the world around us, everything becomes a standard to hold ourselves to.

Sometimes it feels as though my body and I occupy a slightly different plane of existence to everything else. There is me, my body and how we conceptualize each other. We don't always see eye to eye, but our relationship lately has been relatively harmonious. Far from being 'stuck in the wrong body', he and I are in a mutual state of healing and forgiveness. I've treated him so poorly in the past, and apart from the random appearance of lactose intolerance when I was around 19, I have received no punishment for it. One day, with a little help, he will fit me perfectly, and until then we manage just fine. I might not be able to live comfortably with some of my body parts, but I bear them no ill will. It isn't my chest's fault it looks like that, after all.

This quiet cohabitation, however, does not seem to fit especially well with the narrative people have constructed for trans men and transmasculine people. When I was growing up (I say, at the ripe old age of 22), the only two trans men I knew of were Brandon Teena and Max Sweeney. To this day, I've only seen ten minutes of *Boys Don't Cry* – my cis female friend had wanted me to watch it with her when we were about 16, and I lied and told her I'd watched it already. I didn't want to see what happened to people like me, especially not in front of the gawking eyes of someone well-intentioned but utterly clueless. Max, however, I became far more familiar with. He was introduced in season three of *The L Word*, a show about a group of lesbian friends and their relationships with each other and the world around them. The LGBT youth group I attended was mostly made up of queer young women (and I had only just realized I was not a queer young woman), so naturally we had seen every episode and discussed it religiously.

I won't bore you with a synopsis, but I will say that I had a considerably different interpretation of Max than my cis peers did. Framed through a lesbian lens, Max's story seemed to be an implicit betrayal of womanhood, as though he was giving up something sacred and precious that he would never get back. His relationship also starts to disintegrate due to his hormone replacement therapy; he becomes angrier, more prone to violent outbursts as the testosterone works through his system. All my friends saw was a man like me, finally represented in their favourite show. I, on the other hand, quietly wondered if those were the paths set out for me, personified on screen by a tragic loss and testosterone-fuelled hyper-aggression. Looking back, it seems so out of touch with my actual lived experience.

Before they signed off on my prescription, the clinician asked if there was anything that worried me about going on hormones. Not wanting to appear shallow by telling her the truth (it was, and still is, going bald), I admitted that I had heard that testosterone could contribute to increased anger and aggression. I reassured her quickly that it would be fine even if that was the case – I had a perfectly serviceable handle on my mental health, and she definitely didn't need to be concerned about anything messing it up. It had taken so terribly long to get to that stage, and the thought that she might make me wait longer was unbearable.

She didn't laugh, exactly, but her tone indicated that it was something she'd been asked about before. If she had been an unprofessional sort, I bet she would have rolled her eyes.

'Actually, most guys experience an improvement in their mental health after starting T. You might be able to feel a bit more, but it isn't anything major,' she said casually, scribbling something down on her clipboard.

I blinked. 'Oh,' I said. 'Then I guess I'm not that worried about anything.'

And we continued, as though she hadn't uncovered something deep and internalized in me that I had previously been unaware of. She told me she was forwarding the prescription letter to my general practitioner (GP) and sent me on my way.

She was right, of course. Testosterone didn't make me uncontrollably violent; it actually helped to stabilize my mood. The unfathomable improvement in my mental health caused by living as my true self, shockingly, was not a contributor to random outbursts of rage. Although unsurprising now, it illustrates exactly how much of the transmasculine experience has been defined by negative emotions. However subconsciously, I just expected trans men to be angrier.

I knew other trans men, and I knew them to be kind and gentle and passionate and everything in between. I didn't believe that we were inherently destructive. And yet I am still marked by secret biases, I still carry with me those images and fears that were once all I knew. No one wants to admit they have prejudices, but acknowledging them is an important part of understanding what is wrong with the world around us. All I saw for people like me was hardship and death. Is it any wonder my child self's concept of strength was physical prowess combined with apathy?

Absence of 'T rage' notwithstanding, I tried my hardest to be the 'right' kind of trans man. I started going to the gym almost as soon as I went on T, and I bought my first pair of sweatpants to go with some trainers I found for half price at a sports shop. I bought vegan protein powder, which tastes about as bad as you imagine it does, and I still use my shaker as a water bottle. In my mind, starting hormones led naturally to a greater focus on physical health; as my body started changing, I would do my part to shape it into its most ideal form. Trans manhood was defined by the physical; our bodies, how they developed over the course of HRT, was of vital importance.

We started out very strong. I would go running a couple of times a week and to the gym primarily for weight training. Come home, down a protein shake, take a shower, rinse and repeat. I won't say I hated it – to be honest, I do quite enjoy exercise – but once again, something in my brain seemed to shift itself slightly. I realized that I had stopped exercising for my own health and wellbeing and had instead let myself be guided by what I thought would best help me to 'pass'. I was drunk on my newfound ability to move through cis society, giddy with the freedom to enter and exit spaces without feeling inexplicable looming threat. I had never in my life wanted to be the athletic sort. Sports didn't interest me to any great degree, and I didn't even like the ultra-toned muscled look all that much. I instantly retreated, a little horrified that I had let myself be seduced by such binary, cis-normative gender constructs. I couldn't let my masculinity be defined by what suited other people again.

I'd spent six years waiting for the opportunity not to have to spend all my energy convincing the world of it.

In the end, I sort of just gave up. My genetic lottery has left me built somewhat like a matchstick, and I couldn't seem to bulk up, no matter how hard I tried. I'll try a home workout once in a blue moon, but it no longer feels like an obligation. I realized that I was far happier now I could just lift all my shopping bags on the way home from the supermarket; I didn't need to be able to do 50 pushups to know my body was doing fine.

I'm fitter than I ever have been (despite abandoning the gym) but still a long way away from those trans models you see online, posing in underwear with impeccably carved abs framing perfect, barely visible top surgery scars. I had believed that exercise would be the key to unlocking my perfect transmasculine future, that it would kickstart something in my brain that would make it all fall into place. So much attention is paid to the trans body, scrutinizing and criticizing and cruel, that, unknowingly, I had put that same pressure upon my own shoulders.

Far from being defined by the physical body, I feel that my masculinity has instead merged with both it and me, and we finally vibrate at a similar frequency. Not quite in perfect tune, but closer. For now, it is enough that we just exist together.

I also started exploring the ways I experience attraction and intimacy. Without being too indelicate, I have never been what one would describe as 'dominant'. I've never really been the one to approach a potential partner, opting instead to hope, silently and desperately, that they decode my entirely nonverbal signals from across a room and make the first move. I'd always fallen into relationships out of convenience or happenstance; we'd been friends already and they had confessed, or it seemed like the polite thing to do at the time. I had never taken an active interest in my own love life, feeling instead that I had been cast as the romantic interest in a low-budget rom-com.

This, however, did not fit into my preconception of what a post-testosterone man was like. I wasn't supposed to be subtle and subordinate, the datee rather than dater. So, dutifully, I made my attempts. I don't actually have much interest in romantic pursuits, but even my casual flirting felt wooden and unnatural. I hated feeling that I was making presumptions about a person's interest in me, and sliding into someone's DMs makes me nervous. I'm not terrible at flirting once I get into the situation, but making the first move is absolutely nauseating. So that was another 'man thing' crossed off the list.

In a strange way, intimacy was easier to navigate pre-testosterone. At least in queer male spaces, I had a very clearly defined role to play. I was the twink, the sub, the bratty, effeminate bottom with the kind of smooth, young face that attracted men three times my age with no face pictures to message at small hours of the morning, asking for company. I was sweet and complimentary, even though I'd always find myself mysteriously busy whenever anyone actually got around to inviting me over. I didn't make any meaningful connections, but at least it was simple.

Not to flatter myself, but I was actually quite good at pretending, accumulating an impressive collection of clothes that fit my part. Brightly coloured shirts and skinny jeans and glitter, oh my.

Now, my lines have become blurred. In growing more comfortable in myself, I have outgrown the constraints of a role I had assumed I was born to play. My body hair is no longer fine enough to ignore, and there is no way I could stand shaving it all.

I'm endlessly impressed by those who shave regularly, especially now. I can barely bother shaving my face, and that's the part I can see when I look at myself in the mirror. Shaving more than one body part at a time sounds like an absolute nightmare.

I know the definition of a twink is broader than it was back in the day, and such terms are entirely arbitrary, but regardless of the greater acceptance of different body types in the gay community, I no longer feel like I quite fit. I still love the culture, don't get me wrong, but it finally feels as though I don't have to force my way in with a point to prove. My queer identity feels less like a performance and more like me.

It strikes me that this was once again an attempt to legitimize my masculinity to yet another group of people. Subverting gender expectations in measured, unobtrusive ways was just another way of telling the world: *Sure, I may be feminine, but that doesn't mean I'm female.* It's *almost* embarrassing; I see and am in awe of so many people who are breaking down gender norms. You'll meet a few of them later in this very book. They're doing amazing things, and I can't help feeling that I've done them some sort of great injustice. As if I was only playing at activism as a means to an end. I would put glitter on my face and wear a brightly coloured shirt and call it subverting gender roles, but was it really just conformity in a slightly shinier box? I know I'm definitely overthinking it, and there is nothing wrong with experimenting with a style and realizing it isn't right for you. But it's still interesting to think about my own limits and biases, looking back. Even now, a year on hormones, I'm still working up the courage to try nail polish.

I'm laying out the impact of HRT on my identity for a couple of reasons. First, it's because I don't want to waste time with it later on in the book. Although medical transition is an important step for many trans people, it has never been a prerequisite for a valid transgender identity. When exploring trans men and our lives in later pages, I don't want to suggest that testosterone has made some of us 'more' man than others. It's a means of expression, and just because it helps me to express who I am, that doesn't obligate anyone else to follow suit.

Almost in contrast, I also wanted to prove how little it actually made me the man I am. I am more comfortable in my skin in terms of my appearance, but my masculinity exists as a separate and far less definable entity. As you have seen, I naively assumed that HRT would help to solidify who I am or make clear the type of man I should be trying to be. In fact, working to lessen my dysphoria has opened up a hundred new doors, each of them revealing a new and exciting possibility for expression. I no longer feel bound by those rigid binary constructs that had held me hostage as a child. I am not a man because of my biology; I am a man because I am. I am, I am, I am.

So that leaves us, once again, floating in the abyss of uncertainty. If masculinity isn't defined (somewhat paradoxically) by repression and performance, how do we define it? What do we want to teach future generations of men and boys? It's easy for me to look back at my younger self and pinpoint all the things we did wrong. It is much harder to articulate how I would go about fixing it. To try to heal wounds that until recently I was barely even aware of in myself seems like a very daunting task.

I know that I want men to believe they don't have to exist in their own personalized void, constantly pretending that they don't experience life with the same richness as everyone else. That gender presentation is a choice and an exploration, not a series of categories you have to assign yourself before you can be taken seriously. These lessons I have learned (and am still learning) through trial and error seem enormous and incomprehensible, and I wonder how I am meant to lay them out for the world to see.

I need to shift my focus not to my shortcomings but instead to my growth. I've talked a lot about the times I felt as though I failed to be as masculine as I was supposed to be, or the times the values I had assigned to masculinity turned out to be harmful to myself and those around me. How did I get to where I am today, in a state of (relative) emotional wellness and stability? I don't want to brag, but I feel worlds away from the boy I have been describing to you. Not perfect, and not done growing by a long shot, but better.

Part of it can simply be attributed to growing up, of course. Being a child is an inherently complicated and often traumatic experience, and we all come out the other side looking at ourselves with a raised eyebrow and sheepish grin. But, of course, we are not like other children. Our lives – trans lives – come with something extra, another layer to navigate and a world that stubbornly refuses to pay it any mind. Much of what we learn is muddled through ourselves. We pick up bits and pieces where we can, finding ourselves in allegory and inference (at best), but we can hardly be blamed for taking longer to get where we need to be.

There must have been some identifiable factor that brought me here, to being able to comfortably sling an arm over a friend's shoulder with a smile. Something that fostered openness within me – and could do the same for others. It is difficult to turn emotional development into quantifiable data, of course. But I didn't get here by magic.

And then it hits me. Outrageously simple, almost comically so, and yet it is the one thing that had seemed completely out of reach to me during those years of painful and mostly unsuccessful self-discovery. Something that at one point has seemed out of reach to almost every trans person I have ever met. We are so often told that it's impossible for us to achieve, that people like us are choosing a life of closed doors and sick, twisted tragedy. It's sickly sweet and sentimental, and it would have made my teenage self utterly nauseous. It's perfect.

The answer is joy.

Because I did not realize I was a man due to the times I felt angry, or lonely, or not good enough. Comparing myself to others brought me no closer to understanding who I am and where I fit in the world around me. I didn't understand masculinity when I sought physical perfection, or by allowing myself to express my feelings under very specific and guarded circumstances. Being told I had to hate myself to be trans didn't bring me any closer to understanding my identity.

Being a man felt like standing on a small stage in front of a crowd at a Pride event, preparing to perform poetry. There weren't many people there, and it had been so incredibly hot that day that we were all sweating. One of my best friends was in the front row, grinning. I had my battered old blue notebook in my hands, with a couple of pages marked up for reading. It was leaning into the microphone and telling them all I was one day on T and having every single person erupt into cheers and applause. I laughed and they shared in my elation, happy for me and proud of me even though most of us had never met and never would again. It felt like that glorious moment of uncon-ditional love, offered up freely and with total excitement. It was the hug I received from my ex-boyfriend's mother when I told her the same thing, even though her son and I hadn't spoken in months.

Masculinity feels like the minutes after my first injection, when a friend met me outside the GP surgery and I launched myself into his arms, smiling so hard my face hurt. We had staggered back, laughing, and I told him gleefully that I could feel it where my backpack hit the injection site every time I took a step. I think we went to get coffee to celebrate, but that hug is what I remember most clearly. I almost couldn't believe I'd made it that far. Six years of waiting, of increasing hopelessness, and in spite of it all I was here. We don't talk anymore, but I'm glad he was there. Sharing and being able to share that joy has enshrined the memory in my journey to manhood.

Masculinity feels like running for head boy in sixth form. Even though there wasn't a single chance of winning and I didn't especially want to. I just knew that other students had com-plained to the head teacher, and the chance to stand up in front of them all and declare myself proudly and unapologetically was taken with relish. I lost, obviously. I've always been far too uncool and awkward to win something so akin to a popularity contest. But my campaign posters made me laugh, and my friends were proud of me. And I felt certain in myself when I stood up there. Ready to defend myself from the sideways glances and whispers in the halls, or anything else they wanted to throw at me.

I knew what masculinity meant when I was stopped by a shy teenager and complimented on my outfit because I had a Trans

Pride patch on. They weren't able to come out, but knowing it was possible made them feel hopeful. I have never known my place in the world better than at that moment. I felt connected to this person, who had trusted me enough to tell the truth about themselves even though we were just strangers outside a train station. In being unapologetically myself, I had created, if you'll excuse the phrase, a safe space. My identity, and my joy, wasn't just my own; it was the product of a legacy of resistance that was far bigger than I will ever be.

And thus we are brought to the purpose of this book. Because I don't think I'd have realized how many ways there are to be a man without the incredible, diverse and joyous community we have around us. Over the years, I've met a lot of men: handsome men, pretty men, men who wear makeup, men who spend days on end in sweatpants and low-cut tank tops. Sometimes – usually, even – they're a wonderful combination of the lot. I've met people who are men some of the time and all the time. Sometimes men feel especially masculine in certain outfits; other times it doesn't matter what they wear. Men in all stages of transition have come and gone from my life, and each one has been entirely different.

It's difficult to feel as if you fail at being a man when you know that there isn't a singular 'right' way to be one. Joy and freedom of expression isn't a right exclusively gifted to our cis counterparts, and by rejecting the standards that pit us against each other in constant competition, we can begin to see how powerful a community can be.

I spent my childhood only knowing of two trans men in the media, and neither of them left a positive impact on me or my mental health. It stands to reason, then, that the most important and valuable thing I can do is bring our joy to as many people as I possibly can.

I am extremely privileged to have been able to connect with so many queer people in my life, and I am equally honoured to be able to bring some of those stories to the page. The following interviews are conversations with trans men and transmasculine people who are all doing their part to exist joyously and openly. They are all people I have learned a lot from and will continue to learn from for many years into the future. Their words offer comfort and reassurance, guidance and strength, and, more than anything, remind us that trans spaces can allow us the freedom to grow and change.

That, I think, over a decade away from the boy who believed so differently, is what strength truly is. I resist the urge to roll my eyes at the cheese I am pouring onto the page and smile, alone in my grimy student room with my protein shaker water bottle. Masculinity isn't defined by how much we can bear in silence. We can model it on something different. It is our ability to see ourselves and others with compassion and joy, and to use strength as a means to lift those who need lifting.

Even if that person is yourself.

Kasper

Kasper (he/they) is a social media influencer and makeup artist from the UK. They explore a wide range of aesthetics and fashions, with little regard for cis-heteronormative concepts of gender or binary. They use art to blur the lines between masculine and feminine, playing with shapes and colour to produce unique and inventive visual styles.

Right, so first I would like to talk a little bit about your makeup because I think that's what you're mostly known for online. How long have you been doing that?

K: Well, I started wearing makeup as most insecure teenagers do, when I was around 11. I think I got into high school and everyone else was wearing it, so I thought, 'Oh my gosh, I should probably be wearing that.' But then it started to become a more artistic and creative outlet at around 12 or 13 – so eight years, I guess.

Wow! I don't think I ever managed; I think I tried wearing eyeliner when I was 14 and emo, but that was about it and it was really ugly.

K: Oh my God, the iconic emo eyeliner.

Oh yeah, not even on the waterline, underneath it – it was really bad. *laughs*

K: I love that. *laughs*

How does makeup influence your self-expression?

K: I think it just lets me make my face look the way that I want it to look. Because I like my face a lot how it is, but I think it's nice to be able to make my face look more feminine or masculine, or however I want it to look really. It helps me to portray myself to the world the way that I want to.

Yes, because I think there is a stereotype of makeup being for other people, but it makes sense that you have that kind of control over your own appearance.

K: Yeah, that's how I feel about it. It's like I have control over how other people see me.

I love that! So I've noticed an increase in the popularity of the 'clown-core' aesthetic, which is I think how a lot of people have come to be familiar with you and your art – it looks incredible by the way, I really love it. How did you come to realize that was something that made you happy?

K: Most of my teenage years were spent quite depressed. I always thought, 'I'm going to let everyone know how depressed I am and I'm just going to wear all black all the time,' because that's how I thought I should look. I guess there's no other kind of person to emulate because, as a teenager, you don't really see many alternative subcultures that aren't goth and emo. So I figured that I'm alternative, so I must wear all black all the time; otherwise, nobody's going to know. And then I think I was 17 going on 18 and I came into an amount of money. I decided to buy some new clothes for the first time in years, and I went clothes shopping and I saw all of these amazing colourful clothes that I've never even thought about before. I decided to buy some to see how I felt about it, and it actually improved my mental health, being bright and colourful all the time. If you wear black all the time, there's an expectation that you're going to be sad. And then I started wearing bright clothes, and people started telling me that I looked like a clown, and I was like, you know what? Yeah, I'm gonna roll with that. The makeup and everything just kind of came along as a natural progression. And now it's all rainbows.

I like that a lot, especially because I think part of queer culture is reclaiming these parts of yourself. You look like a clown? Sure, I'm going to take that as something empowering rather than letting you use it against me.

K: Yeah! The first time I did the makeup was London Pride 2018. I was in a relationship at the time with somebody who really didn't like that I was getting a bit more colourful. I have no idea why, but I went to Pride without them, with some friends, and I decided that I was just going to look like a clown. So I bought a proper nice outfit. It was all pink and yellow, and I did clown makeup, which was terrible – it looked awful, looking back on it, but I felt great! And I had photographers approach to take pictures of me and people telling me that I looked really nice – my friends said that I looked really nice. I just felt good and decided that's how I wanted to look from now on. So that's what I did.

Oh, I like that! Do you think the playfulness and approachability contribute to the appeal?

K: Yeah, that's how I see it. I have a few aesthetics that I rotate between, but I definitely feel prettiest when I'm in clown. I feel if I look colourful and pretty and friendly, people are more likely to approach me, whereas if I'm in darker clothes and darker aesthetics, I feel the need to overcompensate and be really, really nice to cashiers and servers, and people like that. But when I'm in clown, I kind of walk out and I get looks from people that aren't disapproving. And it makes me feel like they're looking at me for a good reason rather than a bad reason. And kids love it – I love children's responses like 'Wow, oh my God, look at the clown!'

Do you think having such a significant online presence makes it easier to explore your identity?

K: Yes and no. I say yes because I know that the people who follow me are really supportive and really nice. I was very insistent that 'I am a trans man' for a long time, and then in recent years I've kind of realized that I don't really vibe with gender as a whole. So I say that I'm a man for ease because I don't mind it, but I feel I just don't have a gender, and the people who follow me understand that and they get that, and they're fine with that. But then the people who don't follow me, I feel like I'm constantly having to justify why I am the person that I am, and it's not something that I can explain because it's not something that I really understand myself. So I think yes, because there are a lot of really nice people. But no because there are a lot of people who are not understanding and therefore quite mean about it.

I think figuring yourself out online, especially when you're in the spotlight, is a little bit complicated. I do think the internet gave me the vocabulary to express myself. I didn't know you could be trans when I was a kid; it was only through social media like Tumblr that let me explore that part of myself. But at the same time, people can be very cruel online.

K: I feel like the worst thing about it is that some of it comes from within the community as well. I have felt more transphobia from the trans man community than I have from cis people. Because cis people will just tell you that being trans isn't real. And I'm like, OK, whatever, I can kind of brush that off. But then when you have trans people telling you that you're an embarrassment to the community and that you're the entire reason that cis people don't like us? All that makes it worse, because it's your own kind.

Yes, definitely. It feels as though we should have each other's backs a little bit. And then transphobes don't like you either! We aren't going to become more acceptable by tearing each other down; that isn't how it works.

K: Yeah, did you get the approval? I don't think you did. And people always feel entitled to know what I'm doing medically, especially trans people. When I tell them I don't feel the need to disclose it, they always tell me I shouldn't mind telling people, because I'm trans.

I definitely think there is an entitlement, especially in the case of non-binary or gender-nonconforming trans people, that they have more of a right to know your entire medical history and plans.

K: Yeah, exactly, I hate that.

I know you do get quite a bit of hassle online. You deal with it very well. You seem to have a pretty strong community of people who have your back, such as your followers. Can you tell me a little about that experience? How have they impacted your relationship with the community and yourself?

K: Yeah, I love my followers. Sometimes I'll make videos that get this huge influx of hate, especially when I'm talking about my identity. I made a video talking about the neopronouns that I use, and I literally said in the video, 'If you don't have anything nice to say about it, I don't care – just don't say it.' And then I still got a bunch of people saying, 'Oh well, this is getting ridiculous now, blah blah blah.' And I didn't even have to reply to most of them, because my followers did, and told them, 'Neopronouns have existed since the 18th century.' And so they're always in my livestreams as well. They just have my back and it helps me realize that there is a community of people like me. It was only when I joined social media that I realized I could be non-binary and use the pronouns I use. It just helps me feel less alone in my identity.

A community is very important in figuring out your place in this society, especially because trans people don't have a lot of positive representation anywhere, so you don't really know the extent of how you can exist without that kind of positive impact on you.

K: And the thing is, with representation, especially in the media, all the representation is for trans women, and even then it's terrible representation of trans women. And transmasculine people just don't get representation because we're either crossdressers or just lesbians. It's getting better now, but it's still not where it should be.

Yeah, yeah, I talk about that a little in the introduction to this book: when I was growing up, there were two transmasc characters, and it was Max from The L Word—

K: Oh God. *laughs*

*Yeah! *laughs* And Brandon Teena from* Boys Don't Cry.

K: Oh no, I remember watching *Boys Don't Cry* as a kid and I was like, 'Oh my God, that's me, but I'm going to repress that like I really don't know.'

Yeah, exactly. I'm a film student, so I probably should watch it and be able to step back a little bit, but I think because I internalized the idea that that's the future for people like me, I just kind of squashed how it made me feel down and didn't think about it for a couple more years.

K: Yeah. I wish they'd remake *Boys Don't Cry* with a trans actor. It's not as if there's a shortage of trans actors, but they just refuse to use them.

And as upsetting as it is, it's still an important part of our history that I think should be told with some degree of respect.

K: Yeah, I don't know if you've seen *The L Word: Generation Q*, but that is very good. They have an openly trans man played by an actor who is a trans man, and they have a trans woman character who is just existing as a woman. I feel they thought, 'Well, Max is a shitshow.' *laughs* 'We should get some good trans representation in here.'

Have you also always been surrounded by people who appreciate your talent? Because makeup is an art form and it is very impressive. Have you always been surrounded by people who encourage that?

K: Yeah, my family is the best. I was brought up by lesbian parents and two queer sisters, so we're a very queer family, and they have always understood that it is an art form for me, and that I don't wear it because I feel insecure. And even if that's how it started out, my mum never said, 'You should love yourself without makeup, blah blah blah.' Her mindset was always more, 'Well, if you want to wear makeup you can; you'll love yourself eventually, so whatever helps you for now.' And my mum doesn't wear makeup – she doesn't know the first thing about it – but she loves it every time I do any makeup. Even if I hate it, I'll come down. I'll say, 'Oh, I really, really don't like this', and she'll tell me I look great. My family are so cool. In terms of friends, I make a point of surrounding myself with people who have positive energy. I don't have time for negative people, so I just don't tend to associate with them.

How do you think that your masculinity, if you identify with the term, impacts the way that you engage with the world?

K: I feel the biggest one is the way I feel much more at home in terms of my gender in shapeless dresses and long skirts. So I look like a rectangle, basically. That gives me so much gender euphoria, and then I remember that people don't perceive garments like that as genderless garments. Then I have to think, 'Do I want to look like how I want to look, or do I want people to perceive me the way that I want to be perceived?' Because the only thing that I want people to see is not straight. That's my main thing. I constantly have this little battle in my head – I'm trying to work on it – that argues that people are gonna see me as a woman if I wear this, but this is what I want to wear, so it's a difficult thing to navigate. I'm trying to come to a conclusion that it's all just one big performance, so I'm trying to work on not feeling so bad when strangers misgender me because of the way that I dress. As bad as it sounds, it's as though I put it on myself. I choose to dress outside of society's expectations of what men are. And even if I try to look masculine in terms of how I look, I'm five foot two and sound like this. So it's gonna happen. Anyway, I'm trying to work on seeing gender expression as more of a performance rather than conforming to what people expect me to look like.

It is an internal battle between what makes you happy and what everyone expects.

K: I just wish everyone saw it as fabric and paint on your face, and I wish people didn't put so much weight in gendering items of clothing and things like that. Because I feel most masculine when I'm gender-nonconforming. Whenever I dress more stereotypically masculine, it just harks me back to my 15-year-old butch lesbian days, so then I feel like I look like a butch lesbian. I feel more masculine when I'm wearing less stereotypical masculine clothing, and I wish people understood that more.

Cis people just care so much about things that I don't necessarily think matter. Why do you think they care so much?

K: Yeah, there'll be cis straight men who are afraid of wearing pink, and I don't understand why. Nobody's going to think you're a woman because you are in a pink T-shirt.

Did you ever think that you might have to give up all the makeup in order to be perceived as who you really are?

K: Oh yes. There was a whole period of maybe a year when I discovered that I was trans. I found out what that meant and realized that's who I am, and then I thought, 'Wait...but I can't come out, because I wear skirts and I wear dresses and makeup.' I had a whole year of this huge battle within myself, having to give up the thing that I love most, which is makeup, in order for people to take me seriously as the person that I was. And I spent that time hating makeup because it was the one thing that was stopping me from living as my true self. And then when I came out, I really overcompensated and hypermasculinized myself, and I stopped wearing makeup, I stopped wearing the clothes I wanted to wear, and I was miserable actually. Then I came to the conclusion that it's not really going to matter in the long run. So I started wearing it again in a more masculine way, and then I started to get more colourful with it, and eventually I loved it again. But I went through a phase where I just really, really hated makeup, and I hated feeling that way about it because it is my biggest passion and love in this world.

It's sad that people assume that being trans involves giving things up. I think there's a kind of rhetoric that you have to kill off your old self or whatever. But I don't think you do.

K: I think it should be the opposite. I feel that being trans can open you up to the world of gender and gender-nonconformity, and I think being trans should allow you to explore gender more, but unfortunately that's just not the way people see it. They're like, 'Well, you're a trans man. You have to give up every single feminine thing about yourself.' It's as if they view us as two separate people, but I just see it as an evolution of the same person.

Yeah! It's like, 'I'm me but less sad.'

K: Yeah, that's what my mum always says. We talk about me being trans a lot in my house because my mum is my best friend. I love her, she's the best, and whenever we talk about me coming out as trans, I ask if she ever thought I wasn't? She told me that she did for maybe a second, until I got less majorly depressed when I came out, and then she realized that I wasn't kidding. Because before I came out, I was having this crisis about navigating my femininity with being transmasculine. I was just so depressed all the time, and my mum hated it, obviously, because she's my mum. And then when I came out, I came out of my shell a bit more and she was like, 'You know what? This is legit.'

I think it's interesting that the way you and the people around you knew that you were trans is through joy. A lot of trans stories are centred around how we hate ourselves and are very, very miserable because we are cursed to be trapped in the wrong body. But a lot of it is about joy. I think it is about finding something that genuinely is how you become a happier person.

K: I hate the narrative that trans people are just miserable. It's like when people say, 'Oh, you need, they need the worst kind of severe dysphoria to be trans.' But not really. You just need that thing in your brain that tells you, well, you're not really the gender that people have told you that you are. People put so much focus on being trans as this insufferable existence, and that you'll never truly be happy as a trans person until you medically transition in the way that you want to. But that's a long time to spend hating your body! You just have to accept it and come to terms with it until it comes to a time where you can change it if you want to. I just feel there should be more focus on the trans experience with gender euphoria rather than gender dysphoria. People will often ask what I'm dysphoric about, but in my case, that list is very short in terms of things that trigger severe dysphoria. If you were to ask me what makes me euphoric, I could give you this bloody huge list of things! And it's a more interesting thing to talk about, in my opinion. I prefer hearing what makes people happy to what makes people depressed and hate themselves.

Yeah, definitely! I wonder if actually for a lot of us, gender euphoria is what helps us realize and come to terms with being trans. Because I was very sad and very depressed for a long time, and that didn't give me the words to express that I was trans; it was when I experienced gender euphoria and I was like, 'Oh, this is what it is and this is how I fix it.' That helped me realize, so defining our stories by dysphoria is doing us a bit of a disservice.

K: I think it makes it harder for trans youth researching on the internet, definitely. It'll tell them in very black-and-white terms, 'You feel depressed about these specific parts of your body and you feel sad when people refer to you in a certain way.' But if you're feeling sad all the time, you're not going to be able to pinpoint these specific things. Because when I started puberty and I hated my body, I didn't know why. And so when I hated my chest, I internalized that as 'I must want it to be bigger because I'm a girl and that's the only reason why girls would hate their chest.' It was only when I was identifying as a butch lesbian and I bought a really tight sports bra – because I was a lesbian, nothing else *laughs* – and I put it on and I thought, 'Woah...that is the one!'

So how do you deal with the voice that said you have to reject anything vaguely feminine? How did you negotiate with that? And then how do you negotiate with the same voices that don't just come from you but sometimes from everywhere else?

K: I think at the time I was just so miserable pretending to be this girl that everyone wanted me to be that it got to a point where I felt as though I either had to come out or I just wasn't going to be here anymore. So I came out and I got a therapist to help deal with that.

All my trans friends at the time were transmedicalists – really harmful people. Which is one of the reasons it took me so long to come out. When I stopped being friends with those people because I realized that was just toxic, I became friends with more gender-nonconforming people and non-binary people, the sort of people that my friends at the time would have made fun of. It helped me realize that you don't have to put so much pressure on yourself to pass all the time, and then I came to the conclusion that one of the reasons I was so dysphoric about everything, and I was so miserable, was that I was putting so much pressure on myself to look like a man. So all the tiny little things that didn't look masculine enough were causing me so much dysphoria and turmoil, I just couldn't see myself as a man properly.

Then I stopped putting that pressure on myself and started to wear things that made me feel good. And now it's kind of, well, I don't look like a man either way, so it doesn't really matter. I can just look the way that I want to look, and I feel so much less dysphoria now! I don't feel so much pressure to look like a man as I did when I was over-analyzing every single thing that I did and wore, and how I looked. It was down to things like how I walked and the music that I listened to and everything. It was such a horrible way to be, honestly.

I think when you define yourself by all the things you're doing wrong and all the things that you're failing at, it makes it a lot more difficult to realize who you actually are and are meant to be. I remember, back in the day, there were a lot of 'passing tips' lists, and they were all things like 'don't smile and don't move out of the way of people in the street'. Be really mean to everybody and then everyone will think you're a man. First of all, no one will like you. And then it just makes you miserable because you're kind of a prick.

K: Yeah, and the thing is, I don't feel I was ever supposed to be some kind of hypermasculine man. And I talked to my family about my childhood. My mum always described me as a child as feminine in a camp way. I was never feminine in the way that girls are feminine. I was extremely camp, very feminine in the way that men are feminine, in a performative kind of way. And she would always say that's just what everyone's told me and nobody really knew why I was like that, and then I came out as trans and it all made sense. Because I am very flamboyant and very feminine and very camp in the way that men are. But nobody really knew why. And then when I came out as trans and I stopped being that way, people knew it wasn't who I was, and I knew that wasn't who I was. And then I just had to sit down and tell myself to sort it out because 'this isn't who you are. You don't want people to think that you're a straight man. Stop pretending that you do.' *laughs*

Do you think our concept of masculinity is too narrow right now?

K: Oh yeah, for sure. Because people are so horrible to gender-nonconforming trans men, and then that extends to cis men. And there are two kinds of responses to the way that cis men defy gender stereotypes. If we use Harry Styles as an example, because he's quite publicly gender-nonconforming, there are two types of people. You have the ones who say, 'Oh my gosh, you're defying gender stereotypes and you look amazing. You're great, you'll destroy gender roles and all that.' And then you have the other people who are like, 'Oh, I missed when men were men and blah blah blah, and men should not wear dresses and makeup and we should have short hair.' But then somehow both of those people tell gender-nonconforming trans men that they're not really men. So it's like this view of masculinity that we have as a society is narrow and then for trans men it's even narrower.

We're always expected to just be these caricatures of men, when in reality men are so diverse. There isn't just one type of man, so for trans men it shouldn't be any different, but trans men are always expected to be your flannel shirt, beanie-wearing, skinny jeans, no makeup, thick eyebrows, love women kind of men.

laughs How I looked when I was 14, yes.

K: Same! And I wasn't even out at that time. That is who I was. When I was 14, 15 and I was identifying as a lesbian, I knew that the word wasn't right. But I was like, 'Well, I'm a girl and I like girls so therefore I must be a lesbian.' But it never felt as though I was in a lesbian relationship. It took me way too long to think like that. Looking back, there were all these clues. I should have known – my best friend knew I was trans before I did. He's trans, too, and I came out as trans and he was like, 'Oh, OK, that's cool. Definitely didn't know that three years ago!'

Yeah, I do think the concept of a double standard for cis and trans men is interesting, and it's something that I don't think a lot of us talk about. Everyone knows that with masculinity, there are a lot of expectations for men to be a certain way and not all of it is necessarily positive. There's a toxic masculine stereotype, and then people who go against the toxic masculine stereotype, but people don't really talk about how for trans men, sometimes when you start to try to subvert those expectations, people are like, 'Whoa, hold on a second. I thought you were a man!'

K: I think the people who feel most free to explore gender-nonconforming in terms of men are cis queer men. I feel like cis straight men, maybe some of them want to, but then they don't feel they can because there's an expectation on straight men to be really masculine. And it's the same for trans men whether we're straight or not. And he could be a trans man who is 100% gay, but then people won't applaud him for exploring gender in the way that they do for other cis gay men. It's just a huge double standard and I hate that it extends into all trans people. Even non-binary people. They take non-binary people and try to put them in these binary boxes and that is so counterproductive.

It doesn't make a whole lot of sense that at some point people referred to fem-aligned non-binary or masc-aligned non-binary people. Then it was explained why that wasn't really helpful or acceptable, and instead of really examining why people were trying to put those binaries on non-binary people, they just switched to AMAB [assigned male at birth] or AFAB [assigned female at birth] in double changes.

K: Oh, I hate that. But it's as though those are only relevant if you're a doctor.

People forget that I'm non-binary because I use he/him pronouns, and then they'll try to put me into these binary boxes, which we shouldn't do for anyone anyway. But then they'll think that I'm 100% a man and try to put me in these boxes and I'm like, 'I don't even have a gender! I don't have a gender and neither does the dress I'm wearing, so why do you care that much?' I don't want people to care that much anyway.

OK, so what do you think we, as in binary trans people and society in general, can do to better support our gender-nonconforming siblings?

K: I feel like these are just general rules for being a good trans ally. Just stop putting gendered weight on things like voices and clothes and makeup, things like the way people walk or anything like that. We should just stop putting genders onto external characteristics of people because there's just no reason to. That helps to support binary and non-binary trans people, because often binary trans people will feel insecure about things because they're perceived by other people as the wrong gender. It doesn't have to be so complicated, but I feel as though people often think it is.

There's an instinct to look for 'proof'.

K: Yeah, you don't even really need to know somebody's gender all of the time; you only really need to know their pronouns.

You don't need to know the nuances of the way they experience gender. Cisgender people ask me to explain all the little nuances of my gender and how I experience it, but the thing is I'm still figuring that out. My experience of gender changes monthly. If you asked me a year ago, my answer would be totally different to what it is now.

I do think gender is a very internal process. I'm a man, but there's a lot of nuance to what that means for me in comparison, literally, to anyone else. Expecting people to explain what that means is a big ask for someone, especially when you're getting asked these questions by complete strangers.

K: Exactly! I don't know you, so why do you need to know these personal things about me? It's always cis people asking these invasive questions like 'What surgeries are you getting? When are you starting T?' When I know, you'll know. I don't know that yet. I have my transition plan set out in my head within myself. I might go on hormones, and that might totally change. I might get to a certain stage and decide this is it, that's all I want to do, but I then might decide I want to do more than I planned to do. It's always evolving. My gender is constantly evolving. It's like a Pokémon. *laughs* I was girl, then I was non-binary, and I was boy, and now I'm non-binary. It's a whole mess that is always changing, and I love that about it.

Yeah, a mess in the best way possible! What is your favourite thing about being a transmasculine person?

K: Oh my God, all the people I've met! Honestly, the online community of trans people, trans people like me as well, which is something that I never even thought existed. Because even watching trans YouTubers as a kid, there are all of these binary trans people who are quite gender-conforming. And then I met so many people online and there was this massive sense of relief of 'Oh my God, we're the same.' I feel like the biggest thing is just the community of people I'm a part of, because they're mostly really nice and I've made so many friends. They have and will continue to help me better understand my gender and give less of a damn about it.

Community is probably my favourite thing about being trans as well. Just the sheer volume and diversity of people that you meet and see in the world – I would have never had the opportunity to engage with them – and an automatic connection that you have to some very interesting people.

K: Yeah, it's just this feeling of a shared experience with people who I don't even know. I have this shared experience with strangers in totally different countries, and I love that. I also think it helps me to not see gender in so many things. I don't gender voices or clothes anymore because I have so many trans friends. Especially voices, because I have so many trans friends with all these different voices of all these different genders, I just forget what stereotypical female and male voices sound like.

So having this community of trans people helps you to see gender in a totally different way.

K: All trans media tells us that being trans is so sad and so awful all the time, but I love being trans. I would not want to not be trans, and people ask if there would be any difference if I were assigned male at birth. I think I'd still be trans, to be honest. I feel like I was destined to be trans. Even if I were assigned male at birth, I would still be non-binary, probably, because being trans is what I was meant to be. The whole narrative of being born in the wrong body doesn't make sense; I feel that I was meant to be in a trans body. I don't feel like it's the wrong body; it's just not completely right yet. I love it, it's my home. It gets me right where it needs to be. It looks pretty nice. It's just not what I want it to be yet, but there's potential.

Do you think that being trans has given you the freedom to present how you want?

K: Yeah, I think so. When I was identifying as a lesbian or just a queer woman in general, I felt as if there was an expectation of me to conform to what people expect a queer woman to look like. So I cut my hair short and I started to wear more masculine clothes. I just feel there are more expectations put onto cis people by cis people than there are onto trans people by trans people. The experience of surrounding myself within this accepting, diverse community is very different to what it was before. I have this community of super-accepting people, and it gives me the freedom to look how I want. All my friends are there to say I look great and I'm like, 'I know.' *laughs* That's all that matters; I look nice. People in the street tell me I look nice and I'm like, yes.

There's less expectation in the trans community for people to look a certain way, especially more recently. When I was first transitioning and coming out, transmedicalism was a lot more prevalent than it is now, and there was an expectation to look the way that cis people would feel comfortable with us looking.

K: I feel like a lot of trans people forget that being trans as an existence is inherently gender-nonconforming. We're all gender-nonconforming because we all defy expectations of what traditional gender roles are. Regardless of how you express your gender, just the person that you are being yourself is not conforming to cis people's ideas and expectations, so I feel we need to stop putting so many gender expectations onto trans people when our gender is complicated enough. Gender is just so complicated, and I feel that people need to stop pretending they understand it, because I don't think anyone truly understands it.

Sometimes people think we need to take the time to figure out exactly who we are and how we experience our gender identity, and that's the point of being trans. I think there is its own kind of beauty in just not figuring it out, though. It's fine; you can just go with it. It just exists.

K: Just exist, yeah?
   Just go with the flow.

Ezra Michel

Ezra Michel (he/him) is a Los Angeles-based musician who expresses the intersections of his trans/queer identity through song. He hosted the 2019 Trans Pride LA VarieTy Show; performed in Alexandra Billings' I'm Still Queer: A TransAmerican Cabaret, Bob the Drag Queen's Purse First Music Sessions and countless California Pride events; and appears as the first out transmasculine actor on a Telemundo series. Ezra recognizes the need for visibility within his community and offers conversation stories on social media with his irreverent humor and heartfelt vulnerability.[1]

Can you start by telling me a little bit about yourself – who you are and what you do?

---

1   Ezra Michel, Spotify, https://open.spotify.com/artist/5cKZAUUJMK9Ef
    4gUeWoZjz

EM: Sure! My name is Ezra Michel, I'm a musician and a social media content creator; I'm also a hairdresser. I also act and I do a little bit of modeling. I definitely do a lot of stuff, but I guess the main thing that's woven throughout all of it is that I'm a very out and proud trans man. That kind of goes along with everything that I do.

I remember the first time I really felt depressed was because I couldn't bring myself to go to the hairdresser and my mum had to cancel my appointment. I didn't know it at the time, but it was because I was trans, and not having control over my appearance was killing me. Being both trans and a hairdresser must be quite an empowering and wonderful experience.

EM: I do take the responsibility very seriously. I had a similar situation when I was a kid. I was taken to the hairdresser and told them that I wanted something, and then my mom whispered to the hairdresser to do something different. When I was turned around in the mirror, I freaked out. I was crying. My life was just full of those experiences with my hair, but then also it was a space where once I started having control over it, it was where I could find a lot of relief from my dysphoria. Being able to play with it when I was in high school and do my own hair. I had a lot of freedom to mess with my appearance because my parents weren't really watching me, so I had a lot of freedom. I'm grateful for that. When I moved to Oakland for college, I found a barber shop, but on my way to finding a shop that was actually affirming, I called several barber shops that basically hung up on me, saying they didn't do women's hair – and I was out as a trans man; I just hadn't been on hormones yet. It was a horrible experience. And then the place I ended up getting my hair cut was somewhere that I started to work at eventually, and it was owned by a trans man. He taught me, he welcomed me into the industry.

Is that the reason that it attracted you? I feel that styling your hair and having a haircut can be one of the first steps to self-expression for a lot of trans people.

EM: Yeah, definitely. I'm also a drug addict in recovery and so I'm three years and four months sober. But in my early transition, I was also definitely in my active addiction at the time, so all these memories of early transition are also coupled with being very foggy. However, I do remember moments looking in the mirror after a haircut and feeling that euphoria for a split second. Haircuts for me were a huge part of my relief, because I didn't have a lot of it. The times that I do remember having relief were definitely centered around haircuts, because that's the thing that you have control over. It's clothes and haircuts. If hormone therapy and surgery are in your trajectory, but you're not there yet, then haircuts and clothes are really what you've got to work with.

I do remember the first time I got my hair cut short and I was looking in the mirror for so long. *laughs*

EM: Yeah, it's a big deal! I love being a part of that. I've been in many trans people's big haircut moments, which just feels very full circle for me, and very emotional when I get to be a part of an experience like that.

I think there's something wonderful about the way you're so passionate about affirming other human beings. Have you always been that kind of person or is that something you've had to learn?

EM: Oh no, absolutely not. *laughs* I was a self-centered, self-obsessed, arrogant little teen. I didn't have much room for anything but my own pain for so long. And now that I've found some joy in my life, I feel it's only appropriate to give it away as much as possible. When I think about when I was a kid, or when I was a teenager and struggling with my identity, and coming out as gay and coming out as a lesbian, and coming out as bisexual and coming out as non-binary – just coming out all the time – I didn't have a lot of support in the way of validation or affirmation. It was a lot of raised eyebrows, and a lot of 'What does that mean?' So now when I see trans people coming out, living authentically, I just feel it's really important to use my platform and my voice and my free will to do what I want with it and just give people the thing that I really needed that I didn't have.

Yeah, I think a lot of being further along in transition is almost making up for lost time, because you spend so long being miserable. It's like a second chance to be different.

EM: Yeah, because I've been thinking about dysphoria a lot lately and how much of a hindrance it really is. Because I exist with it, I've existed with it my whole life, it just is so normal. But now that I'm further along in my transition, I do have moments where I don't feel dysphoria for like a full five minutes, and it's bizarre!

It's so weird!

EM: I'm grateful for those little moments. We get used to having the contrast that's so extreme – wanting to die and also really wanting to be alive is constantly fluctuating. It just makes me not take for granted the moments that I do get where I feel serene and comfortable.

Being able to just exist is something that a lot of people take for granted, but it is weird when you suddenly find yourself existing in your own body.

EM: Yeah, yeah, definitely. I get emotional thinking about that because it's the bare minimum.

Did you ever feel that the kind of sensitivity you platform and promote now was at odds with masculinity?

EM: Yeah, definitely. When I first came out as trans, I thought that the goal was to be the most masculine version of myself that I could possibly be. I was so focused on trying to reject everything feminine about myself because of my dysphoria with, you know, the things that I didn't feel worked in alignment with my authentic self. But because it felt so extreme and because my suffering was so great, I didn't know what parts of myself I liked and what parts I didn't. I just hated everything. So then I started my transition and I was stealth once I started passing as male. I was married to a cis woman and I identified as a straight man; that was what I existed as for years.

I finally left her because I needed to explore my sexuality, and I had only been with her during my transition. I needed to find out what the hell was going on, because I was really desiring new experiences and experiences with different types of bodies and different types of gender identities. So when I left her, it was as though I had this femme awakening where I realized that I had been so afraid to be myself in front of her, and that's where it began. But then it started getting deeper and I was like, 'Oh my God, I've been afraid to be myself in front of *me*. I've been afraid of my femininity because it was so traumatizing for so long.'

Yeah, that makes a lot of sense. Even before I realized I was trans, I was very anti-femininity in general. I was one of those 'Oh I'm not like other girls.' *laughs* I didn't realize it was because I wasn't a girl. It sounds so dumb now to even consider that if I feel emotion, that means I'm weak. Having and expressing emotion felt at odds with what I thought I should aspire to.

EM: Toxic masculinity weaves itself into everybody's lives. It's not just cis men that suffer from the existence of toxic masculinity and misogyny; you know they're BFFs. *laughs* I definitely had a lot of unpacking to do when it came to my resistance to my femininity and my desire to exist as this toxic, masculine man, who didn't show emotions, and was violent and hit things. Once I started trying this whole radical self-acceptance, it was kind of like a domino effect. Over the past few years that I've been working on it, it really did lead me to get sober from drugs and alcohol, which was a huge issue in my life. I was going to die. So once I got to that point in my journey, it was like, you know, a huge domino effect. And every day I get more and more comfortable with who I am and all the facets of my personality. I'm becoming less interested in trying to understand it and more interested in experiencing it.

I think it's a very cis-centric narrative of transness. There's a focus on how we spend all this time trying to figure ourselves out, but what's more important maybe is just kind of learning to exist within our identities and bodies.

EM: That's been my journey, but I did have to go through all the times when I was trying to understand it in order to get to the place where I found that I don't actually need to do that, you know. So I'm all about people going on their journeys. Obviously, not being alone in that journey – just being able to be honest about where we're at and accept each other in that space. I have a lot of trans kids reaching out to me and asking for advice, and I don't give a lot of advice. I do tell people to be honest and to talk about what's going on. That's pretty much the only advice I give: be honest about what's going on and don't isolate yourself, because dysphoria, suffering, anxiety and depression all thrive in isolation. We're not meant to be alone.

Community is so important for a lot of trans people. When we're by ourselves, we don't often have the words to describe what we're feeling, and then we find this community of people who can give you the freedom to explore that, so I think telling people to be honest is probably a good place to start, because that's how you find other people like you.

EM: Yes, exactly. Honest with yourself, and honest with other people. Things would have been so different if I had been honest from the start; I don't know what would have been different and I don't really care to ruminate on that, but I just think it's a very valuable thing that we have as a tool, to be honest.

Do you think that trans men are held to a different standard of masculinity than our cis counterparts?

EM: I don't know. I can't really say for sure because that kind of seems as though it would be a generalization. In my own experience, I've witnessed a lot of people saying things like 'Oh my God, you're so masculine, you're such a man – will you carry this for me because you're a man?' once I came out, and *laughs* I'm not that kind of man. I know they were just trying to be affirming, but I get it from a lot of people because we live in this society that really loves to reinforce the binary. When I say I'm a man, people just immediately think they know what that means, but I don't even know what that means! I think it's kind of cute and kind of silly, but it can also be harmful in some cases.

I think I've just been lucky in my case because the pressure hasn't been that intense from a society standpoint; it's been more individual experiences that have been challenged.

Yeah, that makes sense. Some of the other people I've spoken to talk about the fact that cis men are allowed to explore more feminine parts of themselves, when trans men are questioned if they attempt to be slightly more gender-nonconforming.

EM: I don't think about that as much. I've been called terminally unique in the sense that I always feel so vastly different from everybody, so I don't really like to look outside myself that much when it comes to how I present. I've always just been super interested in being different and being unique, so when I see society pressuring trans men to be masculine, I don't care. It's my internalized stuff that's the most difficult to get over. Yeah, for me personally, it doesn't feel external. It feels very much internal.

I relate to that. It's taken a long time for me to be comfortable enough that I could even begin to branch out in terms of gender presentation, and honestly, that wasn't anyone else, in terms of society; it was my own fear and paranoia policing myself.

EM: Yeah, and that's internalized femmephobia, transphobia and all that stuff that's been the hardest hurdle for me to climb over.

That's what kept me wearing cargo shorts for so many horrible years.

EM: *with genuine, horrified sympathy* Honey, no!

I know, I know.

EM: Oh goodness, if you would have seen the way that I dressed before I came out as queer. After I came out as trans and left my wife and I came out as queer, my whole wardrobe changed completely that day. In the space of a day, I had to get rid of all this gross stuff, a lot of baggy shirts that I didn't really ever like.

You said in one of your videos that you're so vocal online because growing up there was no trans representation, but specifically for more feminine guys. I was wondering why you think it's important to show that side of our communities.

EM: I think education is power. Visibility in general is so

powerful. If you grow up not seeing yourself represented anywhere, you don't feel like you're valid. For me personally, I didn't
feel I was valid. I didn't feel I could really exist authentically,
because I didn't see myself anywhere. I didn't know that who I
am was even something I could be. And it sounds kind of silly,
but when you experience it, it's so different from explaining it
in words. Because obviously I exist, but when you're a kid, you
don't have a lot of context for the world. So I couldn't really tell
myself that there are all types of people out there, don't worry
about it; I just felt there was something so fundamentally wrong
with me. I thought I should be dead. I should die – that was
where my mind went. Because when I was a kid, I didn't have a
lot of context or life experience.

So when I see people like Gottmik who's a Drag Queen on
RuPaul's Drag Race season 13 in the US, it's just something so
special. I cried when I saw him, because I had never seen anyone
who looked like me onscreen talking about dysphoria, talking
about his top surgery scars, and how he loves his scars. What
the hell, are you kidding me? We had to pause it because I was
completely shattered with my partner. *laughs* People don't
think about it if they grow up seeing themselves represented in
every TV show they ever watch, you know.

*Yeah, absolutely I do. I sit back sometimes and I do imagine if I had
that growing up, and if we had the words to express it. It just felt
that something was wrong and I didn't know what, but I knew it was
something.*

EM: Yeah, definitely. From a primitive, survival standpoint as
well. When your brain is not fully developed and you have

thoughts about how nobody like you exists, it's very easy to make the jump to 'I shouldn't exist at all.'

Do you think that being a trans man has given you the freedom to explore different parts of yourself?

EM: I mean, I don't know what it's like to not be trans, so I can't really say what it would be like exploring different parts of myself as a cis person. But I will say that I do feel very grateful to be trans and to have had access to the tools that I had, to be able to lessen my dysphoria and find some relief, so that I could actually contemplate my identity in a safe way.

It had to go in the order that it went in. I had to be a drug addict, I had to be fogged out and completely numb for my first few years. I don't think I would have survived it, to be honest. I was just struggling so much, and so I really see everything happening the way that it should have happened. I don't believe that everything happens for a reason or anything like that, but I do believe that I ended up here because of a series of actions I took and because of a series of privileges that I have and have had access to. All those things added up to me being able to explore myself. And that is a privilege that I hold very near and dear to me. I have a lot of gratitude for that privilege because I know a lot of trans folks are not afforded the same opportunity to be able to explore. Either the pain is too great or they don't have enough time here on this planet because their lives are taken from them. The fact that I've made it this far to 25 years old and I feel somewhat serene is a huge deal for me.

Privilege is something that we almost don't like to talk about in the trans community. I think it's uncomfortable to want something so badly and then have to admit that it is a privilege when you get it. I think it's difficult, but we are very privileged to be able to sit back and examine these parts of ourselves.

EM: Right, because the suffering is so great that you think, 'Well, I deserve this, so why should I have to think about my privilege?' But that's the reality, and you already made it this far. Why not acknowledge the reality of the situation? It's not going to hurt you. It's not going to hurt me to acknowledge the privileges that I've had in order to get this far. It doesn't make me a bad person. If anything, it's a comment on our society, but it's not a personal comment on me to have been able to accept the privileges that I have as a white-passing, cis-passing, thin, conventionally attractive, educated person in the world. I have all these things that have allowed me a lot of access. To not acknowledge that would not only be doing myself a disservice, but it would also be a huge disservice to the community.

There seems to be a sense of entitlement in some transmasculine communities. I don't know if that comes from the toxic masculinity that we might have internalized, and in an attempt to be taken seriously, we just regurgitate this ideology.

EM: It makes me so angry when trans men act like more trans women in the media is shutting us out of the conversation. There are more than there were, say, five years ago, but why should trans men see that and be like 'Well, what about us?' No, honey, uplift them! You know, if you really want something, you have so much privilege and access, go do it. That's what I did. There's not a lot of representation for guys like me. I'll do it. I'm kind of funny, and I write a lot of songs about it, so that also helps, because people like songs.

People do like songs.

EM: You know, it has been historically documented that people do be liking songs.

I feel that it's very easy to pin all the blame on the toxic parts of our community and acting as though everything would be great if it weren't for certain individuals, but I do feel there is an entitlement that we need to confront within ourselves.

EM: Exactly, that's what it's all about for me. It's all been about looking in the mirror and making the decision to see people talking about how non-binary identities aren't legitimate, and deciding to create rather than sit in that rage and upset. At this point, there's so much animosity between those two sides of our community. I could just start my own little conversation over here, which says, 'Hey, how ya doing? I'm a trans guy but I like dresses sometimes and it's OK.' Instead of even engaging with that argument, I'd rather just start my own conversation so that we can add more spaces. I've had several people who followed prominent transmedicalists in the community DM me and say they hated themselves for so many years because they watched these types of videos on the limitations that we have to abide by as trans people. They say they found my videos and started feeling so much better. That kind of thing hits me hard because even though only a few people have said that to me, those are whole human beings. Whole people, with lives and opinions and potential, and to follow somebody who's telling them that their identity is somehow invalid or other people's identities are somehow invalid, and then to come to a place where they're seeing videos telling them the opposite, that being trans is wonderful, and we love you and see you. It's two different places to absorb information for sure.

I think there's a lot to be said about what is really empowering is not being defined by hate of other people and yourself. I think that where a lot of people become comfortable with themselves is when they realize that they don't have to be defined by this kind of deep hatred.

EM: Absolutely.

What is something that brings you true joy?

EM: Oh my gosh. Well, it starts with me. I have to find love for myself every single day, I have to actively seek joy out because I don't wake up with it, to be honest. I don't, but what I do for that is I dance around in my apartment, I listen to beautiful songs, I sing. Sometimes I look in the mirror and I scream at myself when I say things like 'You got this! You're good! You're a good person!'

And then I go from there. That's a good foundation for me to start building upon throughout my day. But I love connecting with the community. I love the internet – I love the applications like TikTok and Instagram – because it connects me to people. I love creating art. I love creating content. I love joking around, remembering that I'm very goofy, because I forget all the time and then I do stuff and I'm like, 'Oh my God, I'm funny.' Every day is a new adventure for me. I don't have a lot of consistency, but I do have a lot of joy, so I keep trying. That's the thing, I just keep trying a bunch. I don't do it perfect, that's for sure.

*Yeah, but I guess if you did it perfect, it wouldn't be an adventure. I'm not usually cheesy, but... *laughs, fake gags**

EM: I'm very cheesy. I really leaned into it this year, especially at the beginning of COVID. I was really keen on being cool and being seen as cool, and now I don't care. It's a complete miracle in my mind, because that was my whole life. I just wanted to be cool; now I just want to be alive.

Do you think people are surprised when they learn that you don't want to pass as cis?

EM: That's one of the biggest things that people are confused by when it comes to my content. And I think I need to elaborate more on that, because I think that I only feel this way because I do walk through the world passing as male. I think I would feel very differently if I didn't, but at this point in my transition that is not anything at the forefront of my mind, and it's not super clear in a lot of my videos. It goes back to not acknowledging the whole story and not being completely truthful. The truth is if I was not passing, I'd probably be filled with dysphoria and anxiety and panic and discomfort. But the fact that I do pass allows me the freedom to not really focus on passing now, so I'm not thinking about things like how my clothes fit, or how visible my scars are. I want people to know I'm trans. I like people knowing I'm trans. I'm not interested in people assuming that I'm cis, but I do need people to know that I'm a man.

That makes a lot of sense. Again, it's passing privilege – what gives us that freedom to experiment with that a bit.

EM: Yeah.

But it's an interesting thing to sit with.

EM: But also not being afraid to talk about that too, because a lot of times I've gotten messages from trans kids who tell me my videos make them dysphoric. That's fine – I'm not for everybody and that's OK. But people sometimes get dysphoric hearing me talk about how much I love being trans and how much I love my scars. I don't know what that means, because I can't relate to it, but I do believe them. And I don't take it personally at all. I don't think it's a personal thing, but I do think, however, that it's important to express all aspects of transness, not just the suffering and the dysphoria, but also what can come after all of that, too. That's what I try to offer, because the majority of the comments I get are that I give a lot of people some hope that things will get better.

Obviously, it isn't your responsibility to censor your own existence. A lot of my pre-transition self was defined by jealousy, so a lot of that is where it comes from.

EM: Yeah, same. I have this empathy, you know. I don't feel the dysphoria when I see other trans people being happy anymore, but there was a time when I certainly couldn't follow some people because when I would see their posts of them being shirtless, I would get really upset and I would hate my body even more. It didn't give me hope; it just gave me jealousy and pain, so I would have to unfollow people all the time. I'm just, 'I'm here, I'm available if it works for you, and if it doesn't, then please go take care of yourself and find somebody who you can look up to or can look to for help.' That's all that matters to me.

The most important thing is giving people the freedom and the space to have and experience that joy.

EM: Absolutely.

Do you think there is a difference between cis masculinity and trans masculinity?

EM: Yes, I do. If you're assigned female at birth, let's just say; I have a problem with calling myself socialized female because I wasn't receiving a lot of the socialization. I wasn't looking towards the women imagining that I am going to be like them one day; I was looking at the boys, so I do believe that I was socialized male. I couldn't have ignored all of the stuff society was trying to impose upon me as someone perceived as a girl. I don't think it's the same thing as being socialized female solely anyway, but I do think that being assigned female at birth gives me a perspective that either I can keep and take with me into my transition and into this passing world as a man, or I can choose to ignore. I know a lot of trans men who, once they started passing as male, ended up being just as misogynistic as any cis person. So I do think that we have a unique option to remember what it was like or not, and sometimes remembering what it was like is too painful. I've felt that before, but I think that when I remember what it was like to be perceived as female. My masculinity is different – it's calmer, it's softer, it's more grounded, it feels. It feels more well-rounded, I suppose, not so extreme.

We are in the position almost to pick and choose the positive bits of each gender binary.

EM: Yes, and I love that! I love women and I love femmes, and I love things like paying for dinner. I love that, give me the bill, I don't even care if I have an overdraft on my account, I want to buy you dinner so bad. I love opening doors for femmes and all that stuff, but I also love doing that for my six-foot-two partner who is assigned male at birth. This is who I am. It's not just because of who I'm with, and I think that's the part that I can pick and choose. Do I just have to be this way in front of femmes or can I just be this way in front of everybody?

I think it is the freedom to pick and choose that I like about being trans. I like being able to look at the toxic parts and saying no thank you and then yes to the bits that are healthy.

EM: Yeah, definitely. And I'm not always perfect – sometimes I find myself objectifying people, and I have to reel it back and tell myself not to do that; they're a person, they're just a whole human being. I do have those toxic traits, but I do have the ability to remember what that felt like, to be objectified.

Do you ever sit and kind of think, 'Oh, I wish I was "normal"'? Or did you always know that you wanted to be a trans man?

EM: Well, I did wish that I was 'normal' for a portion of my life, for sure. I go through phases. I have gone through phases in the past where I wished that. When I was a kid, I wanted to wake up as a boy; I prayed all the time for God to make me a boy. I was terrified of puberty and all that stuff. Of course, I dreamed of not suffering. But I don't feel that way anymore, not at all. Even on my dark days, even on my dysphoric days, I never think to myself that I wish I was a cis man. Very passionately, no way. I'm so grateful to be a trans man. I wouldn't change it for anything, but yes, in my history, I have for sure hated the fact that I was trans and hated the fact that I was a drug addict. I just hated all of it. It was hard. How could I not hate it? But now I see the value in all of that pain and the suffering, the absolute physical value, because I can see it actually affecting the people in my life and people on social media. I help people because of the experiences I've had, not because I had it easy. So no, I certainly would not wish that I was normal today. Normal in any capacity, with regard to anything about my body.

Sometimes I do wish I was cis, and then I think about what that would actually mean and how that would change me in my life. I don't think you can separate me being trans from me being the man I am, if that makes sense.

EM: Yes. That makes a lot of sense to me at least. I don't know who I would be if I wasn't trans, because there's no other way it could have been. I don't think that trans people are mistakes at all. We're definitely meant to exist because we exist, period. You know?

Caspar J. Baldwin

Caspar (he/him) is a writer and PhD graduate in biomedical science. His memoir *Not Just A Tomboy* explores his experiences growing up transgender in the 1990s when he lacked the vocabulary to describe his experiences. Mixing both memoir and well-referenced scientific evidence, he outlines how much has changed since his childhood as well as the steps we can take to make the world safer for us in the future.

First of all, you're actually a difficult man to research. I don't think I could glean a lot from your Twitter profile other than you have a particular passion for Autumnwatch. Do you consider yourself a private person?

CJB: Well, I'm not famous, and I'm not one of these high-profile YouTuber trans people. So, you know, I'm an average person.

I mean, as private as you can be after writing a memoir.

CJB: Yeah, that's about as open as I've ever been, so I'm not, you know, I'm not a media personality, so I'm not overly private in a regular sense, I'm just not famous.

I suppose writing a memoir is kind of the ultimate not being particularly private. And then there's not a whole lot more you can do, I suppose.

CJB: Yeah.

What motivated you to lay out your life like that? Because it is very detailed.

CJB: There wasn't much for me to read when I was looking in 2012–13. I actually found one memoir written by a guy who was German. I bought a Kindle so I could translate it. I didn't find an English version, it was just in German, so I had to translate it page by page on my Kindle. There were a few others, but they were more to do with an intensely traumatic background that I can't really relate to. I've had a very boring upbringing. Everything was about people who suffered a great deal, but I felt I couldn't relate. So, even though no one is ever going to have a story you 100% relate to, I thought there was nothing. Maybe there are other people like me who were having a relatively 'easy' life, who didn't suffer all these terrible traumas, and that went against this really negative media narrative. When the opportunity arose, I thought I'd go for it.

I think that's brilliant, actually. I think that tortured narrative can make it look to trans kids that there's only one type of life for people like us, and it's miserable.

CJB: Or if that's what people like me are like, then maybe that I'm not like that. It's the boring trans experience that has been left out. I think that's part of why it's important to have this, because the narrative was that being trans comes out of trauma, or that you have to in some way be traumatized in order to be trans. Actually, most trans people are just regular people, who just happened to be this way.

But the way you do talk about your identity is very honest in the book. I found myself a little bit envious of how honest you are, because when I talk and think about my past and my childhood, I feel as though I'm a little bit guilty of trying to scrub the 'girl' parts off as though it never happened, and argue that I've always been this person, but I think when you were writing it, the way you phrase things makes it very clear that you didn't have 'girl' actions or behaviours; it was everyone else that pushed those perceptions of gender on to you. I was wondering if that was something that you always wanted to focus on?

CJB: It was because it took me some time to get to that point myself. In the beginning, I didn't want to focus on the 'girl' parts either, but then I was trying to research inspiration for how to phrase things in my coming-out letter. I came across a website that spoke about this notion that actually you're not the one that's transitioning. Yes, in the body you might be, but your identity is not the thing that's transitioning; it's other people's perceptions of it as a major change. So it kind of flipped around who and what was transitioning. Because you already have that identity; it's just that other people's perceptions of it were now changing. It meant that everything you did in the past was still part of your identity; they just need to reset their concept of what it means to have done those things. Things like being obsessed with soft toys? That's not a girl thing, that was a me thing, and it's OK for that to be right.

I think a lot of that is pushed by the 'born in the wrong body' narrative. You were something before and then you changed.

CJB: Yeah, that was really the only way it could be framed. Now the world is getting aware of the ridiculous gendering of everything, and we're getting a different way of being able to discuss it. It's just an awareness that develops.

I felt especially strongly about the way you talk about your relationship with your brother, James, and that kind of jealous rivalry that was cultivated, not necessarily physically against him but within yourself. I've got a twin brother, so I 100% related to that. Do you think that sense of competition informed how you approached masculinity in the beginning?

CJB: I think it informed my approach and behaviour at the time. If he was good at something, then I made sure I was just as good, because if I wasn't, then I was concerned that people might say it was because I was a girl, or I shouldn't be expected to be as good at things like running or football. Which, when you think about it, is terrible sexism. But it was a weird dual headspace, because

I always felt like I was simultaneously externally sticking it to the patriarchy by being just as good at him and also internally proving that I was a boy.

I think mine was a little bit different to yours because I was two years younger, so it was also harder because I was smaller than him. That being good at things. I was afraid if they didn't view it based on how I was younger, it would be because I was a girl. I had to be just as good.

So you had to push yourself ten times as hard for a standard that normally, if you weren't trans, you wouldn't have had to. There's a standard to set for yourself.

CJB: Well, I mean because at the time I didn't realize I was trans, it was like externally I was doing it to prove that girls were as good as boys. But then also internally when I was as good as him, thinking privately that I am a boy, I can be just as boyish as him. I was doing both of those things.

Yeah, I don't think there's a one or the other. I definitely think a lot of my teen years were spent trying to stick it to the patriarchy, thinking that I can do whatever anyone else can do, and then secretly there's a sense of 'Yes, this means masculinity.'

CJB: That's what it is. It's like, 'What is going on in my head?' *laughs*

Yeah, simultaneously subverting and adhering to gender roles is confusing. But how do you think you've changed from that jealous kid? If you think you have changed?

CJB: I'm much more at peace now. That comes from not really caring at all about masculinity and what other people's views of mine is. You just go, 'Chill out, man, you go on your paths.' Also, James lives in London and I live in the North, so I don't see him as much. But I think since I transitioned, I'm no longer worrying about anything I do and whether people will view it as being a masculine thing or question my identity because of it.

For myself, and some of the other guys I've spoken to, that sense of peace and not caring as much is very important in moving past holding yourself to a certain standard. At a certain point, you become comfortable enough with yourself and your identity to realize that it actually doesn't really matter.

CJB: I think some of it is passing privilege as well, because I do pass almost 100% of the time now, so I don't have to think about everything I do and how it will be framed. Everything I do will always be framed from the starting point as masculine, no matter what I do. For example, if I dress myself head to toe in pink, that's still a man dressing in pink. There's no having to prove my identity.

Before passing, there tends to be a very strong rejection of anything that could possibly be seen as not masculine, especially for me. You so desperately want to prove that you're definitely not feminine in any way that you entirely reject anything outside of the norm.

CJB: I mean, yeah, but it's also as though you're afraid that if you don't, it will be used against you. Back in the day for people trying to transition, you hear those stories about how people were turned away for not looking like a stereotypical version of their gender. So we think, 'Well, I've got to go into my appointment and I've gotta be hypermasculine, there's no other way.'

That was a genuine fear for me when I first started going to the gender identity clinic. I thought they were going to turn around and say no unless I looked as masculine as possible, which doesn't really happen anymore. It probably still does, because that's the kind of world we live in, but it doesn't happen as much. It's still an innate fear that if I don't 100% present super masculine, they're going to think I might be faking, and they're going to stick me on yet another waiting list, you know?

CJB: Yes, I think that will fade as the stories that we read about when we were trying to research about transition will be replaced by our stories. I think the next generation won't be so stressed about it. I went through possible questions they would ask me and made sure that nothing about my answers would be remotely ambiguous. I think I put more into it than university interviews. *laughs*

Was it difficult at all to think about your childhood in such detail? I had to read the first half, when you talk about your childhood, because it was very, very relatable and it got a bit difficult to read.

CJB: Some other people have said that they had to do it in sections. I mean it took me around eight months to write the book, so I did it in sections myself. But I found that it was actually really helpful. I found that I may not have already gone through a lot of these memories before, when I came out to myself. Or I had already gone through them all, but it was really helpful to go through them again just to see situations and my responses for what they truly were. It helped me lay them to rest, which makes it almost like a form of self-therapy. I recommend it. It is painful, but it's a bit like exercise in that it can be hard and painful when you're doing it, but you feel so great afterwards.

I think processing that can be really important, because I think as trans kids we do spend a lot of time being very miserable and not understanding why.

CJB: And I actually think there's a tendency in people who transition to just skip past this sort of work. Because 'everything is great now, let's just move forward', but I think there's something to be said, even if you don't feel you have any kind of trauma, there's something to be said about just taking some time to go back over why things were the way they were.

Again, as I said earlier, I'm a bit guilty of trying to scrub all of that and just skip over it completely. It's only fairly recently that I've started to accept child me as a part of me.

CJB: Yeah, definitely recommend. Especially, because if you write it out, you have to clarify as opposed to just thinking it. Your thoughts can be very fluid, and you sometimes just don't finish a thought before moving on to another one. Whereas if you're writing a sentence, you have to really think about it, so it definitely makes you go over it properly.

Did seeing it laid out in front of you make it easier to accept?

CJB: Yeah, it really did. It's so helpful to be able to look at it and see that this is the way things went, this is how I responded and this is right. I think it was also helpful for people who knew me to read it as well, because those who were there or had witnessed or knew about it at the time could see the experience from my perspective. That was important to me as well.

Yes, because obviously it is published. Seeing it reflected back at you from other people who learn your experiences, was it easier to see yourself from someone else's perspective?

CJB: You don't know whether anybody actually did until they tell you. What has been nice is finding out that other people did experience this as I did. I thought my trans experience was unique among trans experiences, and it's been good to find it actually isn't, in many ways. Which is great. I think I mentioned in the book about the desperate longing to be the same as someone else. The lack of representation is so difficult.

I found it very validating to read it because it was so relatable; I definitely understood those experiences. It was very validating to realize that even if it was difficult, it's not something you necessarily went through alone. We have a whole community of people who are also going through similar things. Has it been a new experience to have more queer people approach you or be in your life in general?

CJB: I've had some nice interactions on Twitter about the book. But I remember, even before that. I have been on the committee of the local Pride group. I've developed a nice community there, but it's still not a lot of trans people because I live in a rural place in the North. There's just not a lot of people in general, let alone trans people. *laughs* But I have met some others, and I've gone into Newcastle a few times and met some people there. Even though you often find that you don't have very much in common with people, just because we're all different, we have this one thing [being trans] in common. It's nice to just be physically in a room with someone else like you.

I think having access to a community does wonders for helping you figure out and orient yourself and who you are, your place in the world.

CJB: If I had had that, I probably would have realized a lot earlier. That representation really matters, but there was no such thing when I was 15. Of course, there was no such thing for gay people either. When I was 15, there were no groups for anything, there was no mention. I mean, this was still the dying days of Section 28, so no one mentioned it ever at school.

You do spend a lot of time talking about how unhappy and confused you have been in the past, but are there any parts of being trans that you feel have had a positive impact on your life or your upbringing?

CJB: I didn't feel that when I was growing up. I think now, being able to look back, there is something about having, as far as it's possible, an experience of life from the perspective of another group – in this case, women. I've been in women's inner sanctums, and as much as I never felt like I belonged there, I was there; I've witnessed and experienced sexism and just the perspective of life. I just wish there was an ethical way for other people to be able to experience that. Cisgender people wonder about what it's like to walk in someone else's shoes – well, I think trans people more than really any other group alive have done that as far as it's possible to do it.

You get this very broad experience of gender and all of its complexity. Cis people don't because they've never had to face what it really means.

CJB: People sit around going, 'Oh, what's it like to be a woman?' and, well, I know as far as I can know. As far as anyone who's not a woman can know, we know. I do wish other people could do it. It also helps you as a trans person to understand other groups we aren't necessarily part of, because we have experience and, as close as you can get, awareness of someone else's perspective. It does help you be more open and aware.

What struck me was the joy that you describe when you realize that there was a word for what you were feeling, and you're not just making this up or you're not just different – there is something there and it's valid and real. I never really thought about the utter relief that realizing you're trans can bring. It makes me wonder how much of the built-up negativity was just confusion and this big question mark.

CJB: Yes, I think so. You just spend so much time thinking whether or not you're insane. *laughs* Or whether there was any point in having the questions because they cannot be answered. That type of question has no answer. You just decide that there's no way you're going to resolve the situation, but you are still left at a loose end. So it was just the relief of definitely having that answer. You can just stop the confusion and the stress about why you're different, and why you feel this way. 'Why am I the only one? Am I the only one?' And you can't even voice that because you think you'll be carted off to some kind of institution.

I tried. I have a friend – I thought she would be the closest possible person who might understand me, but even in our closeness I couldn't voice it. There was just no vocabulary. So you just sit in your confusion for years, and to have it cleared up, even though it's just the beginning, it also felt like an end.

I think a lot of classic trans narratives are very much built around how miserable we are all the time. We hear about the dysphoria and the suffering. But a lot of what makes us come to terms with our identity is the joy and relief.

CJB: It's the joy! It's the movement towards joy, towards resolution, towards being able to just get on with life. I say in the book, it's like you're going through life wading through treacle, when everyone else is just walking on a clean road. And you just, you get on with it, but suddenly that weight is lifted off you and you can get on an equal footing with everybody else. That's the joy.

Especially feeling as though everyone is just breezing past and you're weighed down by this big 'something'.

CJB: Exactly, and you don't even know what it is you're being weighed down by. So you are fighting the strain, and also the strain of trying to figure out why your weight is so much heavier than everyone around you.

So when you know what it is, you can start working out how to accommodate our needs?

CJB: Yeah, before you come to a realization, you're not even able to fight against it. We can't find ways to move at the same speed until we know what can help us.

So how do you feel that your relationship to masculinity has changed? If it has changed?

CJB: I'm less concerned about everything I do being framed as masculine. I'm not worried about wearing pink or things like that. One of the biggest changes was this worry that I had when I started researching queer culture, which was the fact that I'm actually just what would be considered traditionally masculine. You know, I don't present as being traditionally queer in any sense, and I felt so guilty about that. I was worried: 'Am I in some way a slave to this notion of having to be masculine a certain way?'

Then I came to the awareness that it's just how I am. To get to a stage of peace with that was something I had to work towards.

I also feel a lot more relaxed now about my presentation in terms of my relationship to masculinity. I think I was a little reluctant to address the 'traditionally masculine' parts of myself because I was part of circles that would very commonly throw around the 'men are trash' rhetoric, and I may have internalized it.

CJB: Yeah, it was definitely like that for me at the time. There's an idea that you can only be what you are now, but this is part of accepting yourself. You either are masculine or aren't. You have to accept the whole of your identity. Not just the gender part of it, but the expression part of it as well.

In terms of gender expression, a lot of it is expectation. People expect you to look a certain way, and then you have to evaluate and navigate what that means for you as a person.

CJB: You do have to go through a process of thinking, 'Why am I behaving like this? Is it because of me, or is it because of you?' You do have to have that real conversation with yourself. I've definitely gone through that one. I've come to terms with that as well now. *laughs* A lot of it is just kind of being a little bit more chilled out and relaxed.

*Yeah, I think being a teen in general is just being slightly less chilled out; that happens with getting older. Being a teenager was... *laughs* It's a mess. Obviously, we all know that, but I do think, especially in terms of being a trans person, that identity is a lot of just chilling out. It is surprisingly important when becoming more comfortable, just realizing it doesn't necessarily matter as much.*

CJB: Yeah, I think it just naturally happens. You run out of conversations to have with yourself and you just calm down. Then life moves on, because things are busy, and you just realize you've fallen into a comfortable manner with yourself. That's where I'm at right now.

I think that's quite a nice message for younger trans people, because sometimes it does feel as though you're just going to constantly be fighting.

CJB: Yeah, it won't. You won't always be battling. You won't always have things that you have to think about the way you are.

It will eventually calm down. And at some point, you will have peace and the time to just be in your body, and life will just exist.

I haven't really had many of these conversations with people, but I wonder if cis people take that for granted – the chilling out, not worrying about it as much.

CJB: Well, yeah, I think so. They only have to do it once – maybe not at all in some cases. And it happened so much earlier in life. That's the thing I'm coming to terms with, if anything. I'm ten years behind in other developmental, social ways. Because I was so separate from life for almost 15 years, and also coming ten years behind in many other areas of maturity. It's something I'm working on now – just feeling that I am an adult. As basic as that sounds, because I didn't go through real, proper puberty until the age of 26. So when people go, 'You're 31 years old, you should be an established adult', I'm just at that point where you're sort of like 21–22 and you're really getting to grips with the fact that you're actually an adult. That's the point that I'm at. That's my struggle. Now it's no longer to do with gender, it's to do with development as a human. *laughs*

We do start that 'figuring stuff out' stage a lot later, just because things are put on hold by things out of our control.

CJB: Yeah, and we can just be almost stunted. Especially because I didn't transition until later on, and I think it's probably worse the later you transition, depending on how you dealt with it. Because I fully felt as though I just arrested my development in every way apart from academically. I tried to go into this in the book as much as I could, but just in every other possible way apart from academically, I'd ceased to develop. Apart from the way I was forced to develop physically, of course, but I didn't consider that to be legitimate, so that wasn't happening. And something that's massively behind, so that's where we're at now. I'm no longer really thinking gender-wise or figuring any of that out – I'm just racing to mature, really.

That makes sense. My quest for medical treatment and support was and is very long and complicated, as it is for a lot of trans people.

CJB: Mine was very straightforward, which I feel guilty about.

You shouldn't feel guilty about that! It's great that some people have a relatively seamless time. But it has felt as if a lot of my existence, and the existence of a lot of trans people, has been waiting to be you. It can seem like a constant wait.

CJB: It's just waiting to start existing. Something that you will find that when you're 13, you think you need to start existing completely right at that moment, but the thing is, you can't skip that process of maturation. As much as I've tried, this is my recent thing. You can't expedite it; you have to go through the process. And you can't be mad at yourself for not being as mature as other people your age. They got to do it normally at the right time, and I think that this is something that we just don't talk about as trans people. Cis people have no awareness of it; they expect you to be where they are in life. It's like, 'Well, actually, I've only just been myself for three years.'

Exactly! You expect me to have social skills, but I wasn't even 100% a person for a lot of time. *laughs* I think we don't really talk about how it takes time not just to become comfortable in your own identity but to become comfortable in the world in general.

CJB: Because the world still isn't comfortable with us. That comes with the other issue: you can't explain it to anyone because that would involve outing yourself, and if you're not out, then that's the end of the conversation. And even if you are, they just have no cultural awareness for themselves from anything they might have come across in life, like TV, because there just isn't anything. So you can't always blame them, but there's no footing upon which you can start a conversation about it.

Yeah, it's difficult to find the words when there is no way for them to really understand. They don't have the personal or second-hand experience in order to know anything about it.

CJB: You know, we're still at that point where if you tell people you're trans, you might as well have said you have three heads. There can obviously be a lot of different reactions. But I think the most common one is just not to respond, because they don't know what to say. I've yet to experience outright transphobia; they just don't know what to say and they don't want to get it wrong, so they just look at you with wide eyes.

Yeah, a little bit of panic. *laughs*

CJB: Yeah.

Was there anything that you were worried you'd have to give up in order to be who you are? Any aspects of femininity?

CJB: I was only very mildly concerned about fertility. Just because you're made to think it's such a huge decision. It's like, I have to make such a massive decision on behalf of my future self. I'm not really qualified to do that, but it's becoming less and less of a big deal all the time because, you know, I still theoretically retain the ability. Of course, medical knowledge is increasing with time. I still have no desire to have children, but you worry that you won't be able to make this decision.

It was definitely never going to be something that stopped me, but you're always told this is the biggest decision that you have to make. But other than that, I just had everything to gain. I never had any worry that I was going to lose my family or friends. I didn't have those worries. But in terms of things about myself that I might have to give up, there really wasn't anything. The things that I had to give up were the things I wanted to give up, you know? I had everything to gain.

I do remember sitting in the GIC office when they asked about fertility stuff. That's the last thing that they ask you about in the last appointment before you can get prescribed testosterone.

CJB: I don't know what I'll want in ten years' time, but what I want now is this, and that's not going change in ten years. I'm just going to have to be fine with it in ten years, because you have to centre the present self more. I think you shouldn't be afraid of doing that – living the present a bit more.

That is really interesting, especially because, as you said, we spend a lot of time waiting for something to happen. So a lot of our existence is looking to the future, but the importance of just worrying about what you need now is a slight shift in the narrative, which I think is useful.

CJB: Definitely.

All right, so my last question for you before we leave. What do you wish people knew about trans men?

CJB: Honestly, just the things that shouldn't need to be stated, really. That we exist, number one, because that's still a battle. That we aren't lost, confused or otherwise coerced butch lesbians. We know who we are; we are regular people, and we can be any kind of variation of what it is to be a man. Knowing that someone is a trans man tells you nothing else about how they express themselves as a man. And that there's more reasons they might think about their identities and lives. You don't see flashing signs above our heads; we're just out there.

laughs Is that a threat?

CJB: **laughs** We're out there. We are among you.

I always think of that because I grew up on X-Men. I came across the first film in 2000, and I remember that one of the first things they say is that they are 'among us'. **laughs** That's basically where we are.

I was really attached to that film, and it was definitely because of the symbolism there.

I love X-Men, especially when I was younger! Desperately tried to convince myself there was nothing to unpack about it or myself.

CJB: Yeah, that's nothing at all to think about. *laughs*

I feel like a lot of being trans is telling yourself not to think about it for now. That's something I'm not ready to unpack yet, so we will just postpone that for a few years.

CJB: I wish it would change, I really do. The rage that I have now is for transphobes preventing trans kids from being themselves. Seriously, if I'd been ten and I had been aware that there was such a clinic that I could have gone to, and there was a drug I could have taken to prevent puberty, and then it got taken away from me? Honestly, I don't think I would have coped with it. The only thing that kept me going was the knowledge that it could not be stopped.

Then there are a lot of people who are trying to take that option away.

CJB: They are, and I don't know what we do about it.

It's all this misinformation about how it's permanently altering their bodies forever. No one is pumping children with hormones, apart from the thing that puberty does in the first place.

CJB: I think the answer really is to just keep coming out. We just have to. Everybody all the time needs to know how unjust it is, because everyone in life needs to know that trans people are their friends and family. We aren't a faceless monster. I think that's the way forward, but it's obviously still very dangerous. So I'm thinking about that right now.

I'm definitely going to come out more. That's my New Year's resolution as of now: to come out to more people.

Yeah, that is a good resolution.

CJB: Because I'm not actually out at work at the moment. I work in a school, and I thought, 'I just won't go there', but I'm close to going there. I think I'm going to go there.

Yeah, I think that could be genuinely very important for some kids to have that.

Leo George

Leo (he/they) is a poet and artist from the UK. When they aren't knitting, they create art about disability and trans activism with a focus on the intersectionality between the two. They have performed at various spoken word poetry and open mic events and use their work to communicate with members of the community and allies alike.

First of all, hello and how are you, because you're actually the only person contributing to this book that I've actually met!

LG: Yes! We were at a poetry event at the same time, once.

Poetry is something that's quite important to both of us. Can you tell me a little bit about your work, the kinds of things you talk about?

LG: The relationship between you and the people around you is 'performer to audience', and so there's a lot of power in that.

People ask, 'You're not scared to go on stage in front of people?' But going on stage means having the power to be the person that everyone listens to as a minority. I can just stand there and explain clearly, 'Hi, here's some trauma that you don't realize you might be inflicting on people because you don't understand their experience, you might understand their experience better, thank you very much.'

'Also, I'm going to close with a poem about peanut butter, just in case anyone had too many feelings about the other stuff.'

It's a unique position to be in as a performer. I think a lot of people do kind of see it as something brave, because all those people are looking at you, but it's also a very specific, controlled space.

LG: I find it harder to have those kinds of conversations in a group of people where people feel as though it is appropriate for other people to volunteer their opinion. But performance isn't a dialogue in that way. I don't have to be prepared for other people's responses, at least not while I'm on stage. And the people that approach you after you've performed poetry are nice.

So how did you get to a place where you were performing in front of people?

LG: The reason I started doing poetry was I was on a writing course. It was one of those daytime activities for people that are a little bit fragile. *laughs* It was at the local library. The focus was on learning skills, but you were also sort of using it as a cathartic creative tool. That's how I use art anyway. I can use poetry like this. Then, when I was sharing my pieces with the group, both the teachers said, 'Oh my God, you're a spoken word artist.'

I asked, 'What is that?' And they encouraged me to find open mic events, and I was lucky enough that there's a little bit of a resurgence of interest in that kind of stuff at the moment. I just started to share myself, and people's reactions were not something that I was familiar with. I'm not familiar with walking into a space, fresh-faced, doing something that I don't have a huge amount of experience in and being in full control. It was amazing.

Why did poetry click with the kind of work you do?

LG: I think that poetry as a medium lends itself to exploring identity. Especially because there's this gravitas that happens with the words and the style of performance. It's not really up for negotiation when you're on a stage performing; you're just exposing the truest sense of self. You can absorb what I have to say or not.

Do you think that has anything to do with things outside your gender? I know you do a lot of disability activism, too.

LG: I mean, in terms of art and poetry, they are a blend of all of my experiences. So disability is absolutely part of what I create and one part of the message that I talk about in the work that I do.

I've actually just thought of something – sorry for changing the subject slightly, do you mind?

Not at all!

LG: It's just reminded me of when I've needed to use my wheel-chair. In situations where previously people were reading me as male, the moment I'm sat down, there's a gender ambiguity that I give off. The fact that I'm in a more passive physical pose is enough for them to add up what they're seeing to way over on to the side of 'probably a woman'.

That's really interesting – wow.

LG: Yeah, and a lot of disabled men do get forcibly emasculated. Because concepts of masculinity revolve around concepts of power, as a society we actively disempower disabled people. Also, we live in a society that's deeply invested in the concepts of meritocracy. So no one is going to take accountability for contributing to systems that disempower disabled people and make it hard for us to access life and the world outside our own houses. As a disabled person, I don't think people understand how hard it is to be so isolated from the queer community. Everything is a multifaceted fight, and we need to make sure that our space is created considering the intersections of disa-bility and race in making our activism accessible. So there's still a lot of exclusion.

Do you relate to masculinity in the way we would traditionally understand it? Or is there something new and unfamiliar about your masculinity?

LG: I'm currently in the process of recontextualizing and think-ing about the way I understand myself when I unpack what gender is. It's important to question why the one you were given isn't the right one, and that whole journey you go through when you're figuring out which words are the right words. I've identified as genderfluid and non-binary, genderqueer, and maverique was one of the genders that resonated with my experience for a while, which is a strong inner conviction and a clear feeling of gender, but it's completely removed from binary concepts.

Oh, I like that!

LG: Yeah, it is really cool! It was coined by a queer person called Vesper (@queerascat). Anyway, I don't ever feel regret or shame for any of the labels that I chose before I arrived at the understanding that I'm a man. I needed to go through that journey as it was also unpacking and analyzing my concept of masculinity and manhood. It was strange to realize that the reasons I was so resistant to the idea of being a man were the social rules defining masculinity in a very rigid, binary way.

For some people, it feels like a contradiction to say 'feminine man' and then also point out the fact that I'm trans, and a lot of people would question it. They don't understand how my femininity isn't a female femininity. It's a masculine femininity. I didn't pick it out; I just went on a journey to find out how to how to describe myself.

So masculinity is/isn't something confining, to you?

LG: It's really difficult, I've definitely got this underlying desire for people to see me as a man and am therefore placing this expectation on myself to perform masculinity in a way that isn't authentic to me. Then there's resistance against that because it's betraying me and my authenticity, and it's just as stifling as any of the other performance.

And sometimes it's important to do, in order to move more safely through the world. I do feel there's this constant battle between safety and authenticity. That dance that I do between how I want to exist if I weren't being perceived at all, versus how I wish I were perceived, versus how I'm actually going to be perceived. All of these things are playing off each other, and my experience of being a man is within that dynamic and the constantly shifting nature of it, and the fact that I want to be settled in my gender, and I can only do that when I am not responding to the external world.

I don't think that I want to have a cisgender experience, but a peace that comes from just being able to exist is quite nice, and something I think a lot of cis people take for granted.

That's interesting, I've not really focused on the public aspect of transition.

LG: It's weird, the pandemic has come at a really weird time. I'm going to come out the other end of it with some semblance of facial hair, so I'm going to have more visual signals to some people that I am a man, as far as they are aware of what a man is.

I'm not experiencing this part of my transition to move in the same way, because I don't have a public life in the same way that I would outside of the plague. *laughs*

Do you think it is more internal than it has been in the past? Because you have the time now to experience it on a personal level rather than everyone else seeing it [physical transition] as it happens.

LG: I did say something in therapy that my therapist said we need to come back to. I said that I can't imagine who I am if I'm not being perceived. *laughs* I'm like the light inside a fridge – my concept of myself is so tied up in other people's perception of me, and whether or not I feel that they're right, my whole life is just trying to calibrate that and make sure other people's perception of me is a reflection of actual me. There's definitely some work to be done to extricate myself from that process where I'm constantly trying to balance myself based on other people and let go of the need.

The goal is to let go of the need for other people to understand me.

A lot of people consider things 'traditionally feminine', such as doing makeup and dressing a certain way, as a rejection of masculinity. It seems less a rejection of masculinity and more a kind of extension and exploration of its potential because that's how you experience it.

LG: I do tend to get the most joy from how transgressive people perceive my masculinity to be, when it's a blend of masculinity and femininity. As far as other people categorize things like makeup and the tone of your voice and the way that you move your hands when you talk and your interests and the things that you're into. But no, I'm just... I'm soft. I'm caring and compassionate, I'm creative. I am very aesthetic driven.

laughs Oh, that sounds pretentious. You should never go to art school.

But I have this body – why not decorate it? There are things that I can do that make me enjoy my body more – why wouldn't I? I can't really get that into some people's heads. They think that if you're a man, then you should be embracing toxic masculinity. But that's not what being a man is. Yes, I'm a man and I know how to put lashes on! *laughs* Although, to be quite honest, that is something that I only really mastered last year.

I definitely did go into that deep masculine identity as a way to kind of deal with my dysphoria. To be quite honest, I think that it's just something inherent in me that I can't run away from. I always look like some level of androgyny. Before HRT, people weren't perceiving my body to be that of a cisgender man. No matter how masculine I tried to look, I just looked like a lesbian.

That can be really hard.

LG: Yeah, growing up, I remember just being obsessed with other gender-nonconforming people. It was just, 'Oh, you fuel me and I don't understand why.' And then even at university in my 20s, when I was going through the biggest wave of no visible dysphoria. I went through my journals a couple of years ago from when I was in uni, and there's like an entire page where I'm so aggressively scratching into the page that I ripped it with the pen, that tells myself that I don't want a sex change, stop obsessing over it, calling myself a freak.

It was shocking, honestly, because I don't remember feeling that way. I don't remember being that violent to myself. So I will say part of the joy that I derive from being androgynous, and having non-traditional masculinity or having a more playful and creative approach to expressing my masculinity, is that I am regaining some amount of power and control. I have a body that has received so much violence, physical and otherwise, and this is how I take it back.

That's so empowering – thank you so much for sharing!

LG: I think there obviously is a deliberate erasing of our history that is partially to blame, but we do have a very long and complex history that exists and is out there. But we have to write our own because it has been kind of systemically dismantled. Which is why I think, specifically in the trans community, it is so important to be sharing stories and being public about identities because we don't have much of a traceable history to show that this conversation has been going on for generations. People have always been talking about how much of gender is an authentic experience and how much is a performance. Hopefully, the louder we get, the more widespread we get with having conversations that challenge and deconstruct the idea that there is some sort of scarcity of human rights, and hoops you have to jump through to please your oppressors and in order to be allowed your slice of the pie. The only reason that people have their rights withheld is that the people have the power to withhold your rights. It is never the fault of your own community for not performing the way you think they should.

It's strange, because for a long time I thought the way I viewed my masculinity as very angry and volatile was entirely self-imposed, or just part of who I am. But talking to people like you has made me realize that actually a lot of it was just how society expressed masculinity to me, not how I expressed masculinity. Did you ever think that there was a way you had to act? More/less stereotypically masculine, more/less stereotypically feminine?

LG: Trying to act in ways that people consider stereotypically masculine is difficult, because it's things like not smiling, or being cruel to people. It feels like not just a betrayal to who I am as a person but a betrayal to all of the women in my life and the feminist work I've done that was a precursor to unpacking my concept of gender entirely. Because I was already doing the work and managed not to get sucked into TERF [trans-exclusionary radical feminist] rhetoric. For a couple of years, I had people messaging me, thanking me for being such a good trans ally *laughs* and I would reply, 'Oh, I'm closeted, too!'

I think before I even came out to myself, I was definitely trying to navigate moving through the world in a more confident way, and I did try a lot of those techniques, like keeping your head up, pulling the shoulders back and staring straight ahead – don't make eye contact. That's the kind of stereotypical behaviour in men, their entitlement to the space around them, their unquestioned and unchecked entitlement to the space around them. But I don't think I would have found that affirming to my gender, because that only felt powerful when people perceived me as femme. The moment that people started to perceive me as masculine, that felt almost violent.

How do you work around the idea that you're embracing something 'bad' in masculinity?

LG: Being trans in this world is an experience, yeah, but I can't perceive myself in any other way, and I don't want to not be trans. I can't understand who that person would be. We are the culmination of all our experiences; that's what makes us people. All the things that have happened in our lives, and the ways that we've responded to them. I can't say with any certainty obviously, but I do think that if I had been assigned male at birth, I would still struggle with conforming to the gender that I'd been assigned, and I would possibly identify as genderqueer and non-binary if I had been assigned male at birth.

laughs You're not the first person who's said that to me in this book!

LG: I think my mom had an impact on my perception of gender. She was a feminist in the 1980s, and she definitely unpacked a certain amount of gender conformity, and she went to women-only DIY classes so that she could learn to lay carpet and put up shelves, which was obviously wonderful – being poor and having those skills means you have a huge amount of control over the comfort and usability of your space. But I don't think she's done the amount of work that needs to be done in order to expand beyond the ways gender roles are harming people, too.

It took her a while to wrap her head around the fact that I'm not a woman. I don't really bring it up now; I just think, OK, as long as she can still interact with me like I'm the same person, which she's just about got her head around. My mom made a real effort to bring my sister and me up in as gender-neutral a way as she could conceive of, but for her that was swinging hard away from soft and pink and fluffy and girly.

I really wonder how it's so difficult for her to perceive me as not a woman if she, you know, if she was very happy to steer me away from traditionally feminine things in the first place. And now I'm more feminine than my sister! I wonder how my mom would have raised a boy. She thought she was raising two girls; I wonder if she would have provided more pink and girly things if she had raised a son. I might have had that space for the first seven to ten years of my life, where I really didn't understand that I had a gender. I was never forced to be feminine; I picked up external messages obviously, but at home I wasn't forced to perform girlhood in a way that I think a lot of other people were. I wonder if she would have made space for me to be a feminine boy, and I wonder if that would have been a more successful and more authentic gender experience growing up – to allow me feminine stuff within the context of being a boy.

I think we spend a lot of time with a kind of 'smash the patriarchy' sentiment – and obviously yes, very true and good – but do you think that impacts how we're allowed to explore the male parts of ourselves?

LG: Honestly, yes, but what makes me sadder is when it comes from our own community. There are too many trans men who have this idea about what a man is and should be, and if you don't try to emulate cisgender masculinity, then you aren't really trans.

You end up holding yourself and literally everyone around you to this impossible standard. If you're defined by hatred for everyone else, and also yourself, that becomes your entire existence, which is horrible, and it makes me sad.

LG: And they will get a sense of community because there will be shared experiences, and if it's the first time they've found people that share that, it can validate some of the stuff that they're experiencing. That is where they're going to feel safest, and so they maybe aren't going to be as critical about the really toxic ideas that also come hand in hand with that. For so long, trans people – or queer people in general – have had the way that we live our lives dictated by the cis-het majority and they require us to hate ourselves in such a way that we emulate their way of being – instead of exploring ourselves and our authenticity, how we are, what we need and what we want. I don't know what the right approach is to combat that other than just openly thriving in all my trans glory to show other people that there's an option that you can be happy.

I think it's interesting that you bring up that a lot of the vitriol is because transmedicalists and trans people who are often aggressive to non-binary or gender-nonconforming trans people come from a place of safety.

LG: They've partitioned themselves off in their own community, and there isn't a lot of overlap really between these very separate queer spaces, where it's very binary and toxic, and all blending into cis society.

I agree. I do think that such distinct groups make it difficult to have these conversations, because although that kind of rhetoric isn't some-thing I subscribe to, I do understand where it comes from. When you don't have the words to explain why you're so miserable, it's easier to project that hate outwards and blame everyone else.

LG: Yes, because these kids really hate themselves. And they're doing what they need to do to survive in a world that says it won't accept you unless you fit this narrow box. They think that they have to be a certain person to be allowed to exist at all, and so they get so angry at people who aren't acting that way because they hold themselves to this impossibly high standard.

So masculinity is/isn't something confining, to you?

LG: I can't conceivably imagine a version of myself that doesn't break a significant number of binary rules about gender – that version of me just doesn't exist, and if it does, it's very, very repressed. The thing is, cis people don't actively engage with their gender. They don't experience their gender in a way that they could – and they definitely could! It's an opportunity that's open to them. They could be curious about their gender, question it and explore it, and come out the other side with a deeper understanding of themselves as a cis person. Until we have a society where it's not taboo to just have an exploration of your gender, I think a lot of these people will have quite a flat and shallow experience of gender.

I think we're lucky to be trans; I think there's something quite special about having this power and ability to understand these nuances in a way other people don't.

LG: It's really interesting. There's a huge amount of overlap in terms of concerns about how white, cis heterosexuality encounters patriarchy and how damaging that is to the world and how much trauma it inflicts on people. It's just important to remember that excluding trans people from the conversation is not the way that you're going to solve that problem. People get scared and they get lied to about what the real issues are.

Once we realize that they're entirely self-imposed, it gives us freedom to explore the parts that work for us personally.

LG: There were times, there are times that I look back on, and I was like, 'I clearly knew you, but I didn't have any context.' You can't take action on something if you don't really understand it. It's just confusing and miserable, and nobody is going to make it make sense unless we let people explore themselves at their own pace and time.

Colton Gibbons

Colton (he/him) is a PhD student and personal trainer from the USA. He runs fitness classes both in-person and online, with a focus on an inclusive and welcoming environment for people of all backgrounds and levels of fitness. He is in the process of trying to set up his own organization centered on people of color in the fitness sector.

Hi! Would you like to introduce yourself?

CG: Sure! My name is Colton Gibbons, I go by he/him/his. I'm currently a PhD student studying business psychology. I actually finished my masters in sports management last year, and the work that I'm doing currently and within the academic space works on targeting historically underrepresented communities. I focus on the trans BIPOC [black and indigenous people of color] experience, which also definitely digs a little bit deeper into the immigrant narrative and those who don't always have the same access to resources as most people in America.

All of that intersects completely with what I do for my nonprofit, which I recently started, which looks at the trans BIPOC experience and figuring out how can we better serve that community through creating jobs, providing opportunities and leadership. It also considers what resources the community actually needs, and how I can better serve that community and facilitate dialogue with other people for better understanding for everyone.

Your nonprofit is Cake Society Co, and it's the first BIPOC, trans-led fitness nonprofit of its kind, which is incredible. Can you tell me a little bit more about that and why you think it's so important?

CG: I've been in the fitness industry since I was around 18–19 years old. I've worked for all-women gyms, I've worked for gyms that focus on a very specific income range, I've worked in gyms that kind of focus on other income ranges and different demographics, and throughout my entire career in personal training and fitness, I've seen the exact same theme running through the fitness industry, which is 'We are here to push a specific body image and specific goal.' This is regardless of what their goals actually are, and it is, in my personal opinion, completely exclusive to those who might not even have these types of goals in mind in terms of what they want to do with themselves and what their bodies are like. So to have a company that is now going to focus on being able to provide equal access to the same type of high-quality physical and mental health benefitting experiences is something that I think is not only revolutionary, but it's just a need in our community. There have been so many different gyms that have accommodated specific demographics – predominantly for-profit companies – that to actually have a nonprofit which ideally will have corporate investors or donors as well as having grant money behind it, which also has historically gone to other demographics, should be something that is not just a blatant need, but it's answering the question, 'Why hasn't this been done before?'

There does always seem to be an assumption that you will have the same goal in mind that 'everyone else' does, and that is to fit into a very specific body type. Is your work more about personal needs? For example, do you focus more on emotional wellness rather than, say, losing weight?

CG: Yep, absolutely! Something that's really important to me is to also incorporate the basic psychology of what our motivators are, what makes us happy and what brings us a sense of satisfaction. For a lot of people, that could look like just literally moving their body in a way that's going to bring them joy, or moving their body among others, and dance classes, fighting classes, group fitness. What's most important is having that ability to be a part of a community and to feel at home, to feel safe and to feel that there is no reason why somebody shouldn't belong in an environment, and to have that mental health as well as physical health connection is something that's really important to me. I think both of them go hand in hand, but to have an environment that specifically and explicitly allows for that to happen is something that you don't see too frequently in the fitness environment.

For trans people, our identities can be very tied up in how we view our bodies, so rather than focusing on fitness in the literal sense, it can actually be a way for people to get control over how they perceive themselves.

CG: Yeah, and also just for the sole benefit of you. You know, being able to, whether dancing and expressing your body in a certain way, it's just being able to have the option of doing it and know that this is an environment that's welcoming and also will accommodate needs that normally aren't listened to.

I think we tend to center white trans bodies, especially in terms of what we consider desirable. How do you think that impacts what we consider 'masculinity' to be?

CG: I 100% resonate with that. You know, I hate the terminology of passing and I feel like there's this weird passing dichotomy that takes place, in health and wellness as much as any other field. I think that either for those who English is not their first language, or if they're from BIPOC experience, or even if they just don't consider themselves to have the same social status as those in a white, cis-normative society, there is definitely a lot of exclusiveness. Even within the trans community, and I've faced that from my own lived experience plenty of times, and trans fitness chat rooms or trans Facebook groups where it's pretty clear that I could post the exact same photo as somebody and the amount of engagement is so substantially different! It's just blatant marginalization, even within our own community.

And unfortunately for our community, as so many of us know, it takes so much strength and courage to get out of bed, to live authentically, to be able to call ourselves our name that we genuinely resonate with. How are we supposed to form a business for profit? How are we supposed to get an education? How are we supposed to even get a job or be able to step foot outside our door? So I just know that there's very clear privilege that is required to kind of be able to do something like this, to serve specifically the BIPOC community, and I just want people to know that wherever they are and whatever walk of life, whether BIPOC or not, whether English-speaking or not, this is an environment that is very much inclusive to all and centered around those who might not have necessarily had the voice that they've needed throughout their transition, and whatever that looks like for them.

It can be difficult to think that you are able to take on a leadership role when it is so difficult to just go outside sometimes. I think a lot of trans people (and cis people, honestly) struggle with fitness/ working out as a concept, and it can be difficult to find a balance between actual health and wellbeing and this idea that we're meant to use fitness to look a certain way. Have you ever found it hard to navigate that, and, if so, how?

CG: Absolutely. I've always been involved in fitness for a few different reasons. One of the first ones I realized was that, being diagnosed with ADHD [attention deficit hyperactivity disorder], I've always had ample amounts of energy, and I would say a passion and curiosity to kind of exert myself in multiple different areas of my life. And then when I realized that fitness was a way of actually being able to take control of some of this extra passion and extra energy, I've always just kind of leaned on it to be able to give me that. But what I will say is, prior to transitioning and prior to coming to terms with myself, I did use it 100% to masculinize my body the way I've always thought I wanted to look. By the time I did transition and I was able to take the steps that I wanted, I realized that fitness was a way of giving back to myself not just physically but mentally as well because it pushed me to new goals. Now, I feel that I'm actually giving myself some type of gift – through mental health wellness, through physical wellness. I was only able to achieve that through actually working out for myself, rather than other people. I think there's so much that wellness, that fitness can offer. If you offer community, if you offer goals, it could offer mental health wellbeing, and can offer some type of personal achievement or some type of personal space where somebody could feel like 'I am doing this for me, I'm doing this for my body', whatever the outcome is, whatever the outcome or whatever these goals or results or the expected outcome is. I do think that fitness can be a way of giving back to your body. Whatever fitness means is something personal and should be up to someone to determine, and it shouldn't be up to some fancy gym to tell you that you need to look this way, or this is what men look like.

Your classes are very much about creating a safe, inclusive space, so do you kind of run queer-centric events often?

CG: I definitely started with that idea, but what I did find is that, in the best way possible, the more that COVID-19 restrictions relaxed and people were actually able once again to set foot outside, be happy in the sun and enjoy each other, I got a lot more people from every walk of life. I do bring a lot of my friends often who are of the trans experience, and then on top of that, I do work within a lot of different partnerships and different organizations, which are either trans-related or queer, that work to raise money. Those classes are obviously usually packed with people of queer and trans experience. So yeah, I do what I can. I will say, probably as we further develop the nonprofit, I think that the classes are definitely going to start shifting and we're going to be able to, in a beautiful way, see a lot of different faces from different communities. I'm really excited about that. And hopefully they will become more queer-centric, just to continue to serve the community.

Fostering this sense of community both in real life and online [Colton has been continuing his fitness classes via Zoom during the COVID-19 pandemic] is something very important to you, then.

CG: Yeah. I think for me it's just because you know nobody wants to be the only trans person in the room. I usually am in a fitness setting. You know that all these people here do what they're doing and I'm doing what I'm doing, but I don't need somebody scrutinizing why I'm doing it this way and why I'm using something like this. I just want people to know that there's nobody here to scrutinize you. You shouldn't feel like you have to lift heavier or stop anything you're doing just so we train you a certain way. It's just something I've experienced a lot of, and I've also looked into a lot of people who specifically don't like to put themselves in certain settings because they just feel there's no community. There's no way for them to relate to anybody else.

Sometimes going to the gym in itself for trans people can almost be quite isolating, because you do feel like the odd one out in the changing rooms, or it feels as though you can't do as much as other people because it might draw too much attention to yourself, but the idea that you've created a space where you can just do what you are capable of and what you want to do must be quite empowering, both for you as the creator and your participants.

CG: One of the biggest motivators for why I'm doing this is because I'm taking a look at, here in America, what gyms advertise as their LGBTQ+ inclusive policies versus their actual capitalistic outlook, and it's quite insulting that a gym wants to take a look at you and tell you that they are the most LGBTQ+ inclusive gym, they are a space that promotes equality, yet their barrier to entry is $120+ per month.

If you are LGBTQ+ inclusive, you would know that our community experiences poverty rates of over three times the national average.[1] You know that homelessness, experiencing moments of food instability, experiencing so many different factors that actually contribute to people being unable to afford more than, say, $10 a month. You say that people are only able to participate if you can afford something that is, essentially, part of a very specific tax bracket. You shouldn't even take the honor or the privilege to say that you're LGBT inclusive, in my opinion. They're saying that you can exist freely in this safe place,

---

1   M.V. Lee Badgett, Soon Kju Choi and Bianca D.M. Wilson (2019) 'LGBT Poverty in the United States.' Williams Institute, UCLA School of Law. Accessed on 13/01/2022 at https://williamsinstitute.law.ucla.edu/wp-content/uploads/National-LGBT-Poverty-Oct-2019.pdf.

but you have to be able to afford X amount. That was one of the biggest reasons why I wanted to do this, and also have people acknowledge that these places sometimes aren't safe spaces. These aren't places that serve everybody. Spaces aren't inclusive if they only let you in as soon as you're privileged enough. If you can't afford them, then you have to go continue to work out in the street, where you're at risk of being murdered, marginalized, harassed, victimized. The whole nine yards.

That's such a good point, to think about the intersection of identity and the fact that to be able to move through these spaces is an intense privilege, and the fact that you do run this nonprofit is important not just from a safe space or surface level, because you're around other queer people, but it's also that for-profit gyms are inherently privileged spaces, right? Is that something you've learned through your own personal experience? Or has it developed just being a part of the wider queer community and seeing the issues that we face? Is that something you always wanted to platform?

CG: I think it's honestly a combo of everything, because as I was trying to try and confirm this, I was thinking about my lived experience with gyms where I've personally been made uncomfortable, in terms of locker rooms, or gyms that I know, and I also know what the barrier to entry actually looks like normally compared to when Pride Month rolls around, who's opening their mouth versus what they're actually doing to facilitate the needs of the community, and I think all of it kind of piles up and I just thought, 'That's enough.' Somebody needs to do something about this. That urgency or that personal call to action that I felt is what really made me get this started.

Has the focus on community and the importance of serving your community impacted how you perceive your own masculinity and masculinity in general?

CG: That's a great question! Yeah, 100%, because the more I became comfortable with myself, and the more that I was able to experience my own authenticity, I think the more I was able to come to terms with how identities can be very complex. I identify pretty strongly as transmasculine versus, for example, 'traditional man'. I very specifically use the version 'transmasculine' because for me, yes, I do use he/him/his pronouns, and if there is something that's going to come out of your mouth to call me or to approach me, I would have a strong preference for 'man'. But that being said, I don't necessarily feel for me personally that I am the traditional masculine male of America. That is not what I've ever needed to be. That is not how I've identified my masculinity within the realm of what provides me happiness and how I can express that through action, clothing, through an effort to be honorable as an individual.

Honestly, in terms of masculinity, whatever that means to anybody else, to me it tells me that I just need to be a better person and figure out how can I assist everyone else and how can I use my privileges to better serve my community.

At the beginning of my transition, I spent so much time on masculinity as everyone else understood it. I wanted to be myself, at any cost, and that was far too much in terms of who I am now. I don't think I was wrong, necessarily; in the beginning, I was so intense because I needed people to stop misgendering me and stop calling me my old name, so I was asking myself what I could do to have people respect me. I do not need that now.

I did not need to be identified as hypermasculine because that isn't who I am.

I definitely also think that I was so desperate to not be misgendered that I would veer all the way to hypermasculine. Pretending to be a girl is difficult enough, and then you just kind of flip to the other end and you're performing this masculinity in a way that isn't authentic to yourself. But a masculinity that is incredibly healthy is a masculinity that is informed by caring for other people. In fact, very much where you seem to be coming from is a masculinity informed by care for yourself and care for those around you.

CG: Yep, exactly.

Do people tend to expect your version of masculinity to be more traditional than it actually is? When I think of male fitness, it is very much focused only on getting stronger and bench pressing whatever. *laughs* The fact that you come from almost the opposite side, does that surprise people?

CG: I would say it does. I think unfortunately I have experienced some exclusiveness actually from the community because of false assumptions. I'll be transparent: once I'm organically in my house, it's a lot of effort sometimes to get dressed up. So I do definitely take a lot of pictures or videos without a shirt, because that is just exactly how I am in my house. Also, I waited for 24 years of my life to take my shirt off in the general public, so now I'm able to take it off, I'm going to. I had a surgery called peri, or peri areolar, that my insurance covered fully, and I had a surgeon in my very local area. I feel extremely lucky for that.

And for a lot of trans people and gender-expansive folks, we lean on our comrades to figure out things like 'What does your body look like now?' 'Could my body possibly look like this?' But there's this very weird relationship that occurs when people talk about top surgery or they talk about what goals we all have. We all have scars, whether they're visible, whether they're more visible than others. But some people say I'm not trans enough based on what my surgery resulted in, and it's kind of like, 'Well...I am, as you are. I am taking my shirt off as I have wanted to do my whole entire life. I don't really know how else to better accommodate you, but I want to be included in the trans experience as I am. I feel I should deserve that pride in my body, and unfortunately I do feel like I've experienced some weird relationship with the community where it's as though I'm not being trans or gender-expansive enough because of what my body looks like. I'm not here to tell you to get a certain surgery. I'm not here to tell you to get any surgery. I am just trying to live my life authentically.'

In terms of what surprises people, I experience my masculinity differently from everybody else. Everybody experiences it so immensely differently, and people get sensitive about their surgeries, and they get sensitive about their lives. I feel the same way, and it's kind of shocking to people. It shocks people when I say that I have insecurities, because it looks like I'm bragging or only presenting one kind of trans body.

It's frustrating, because to be trans and gender-expansive for me has always been about the need to accommodate others. Someone with our shared and different experiences should always be held in that same type of high regard, and we have a duty to welcome people and make them feel invited and that they are trans enough. Whatever that means to them.

I wonder if it's almost a jealousy thing, because when you have peri, the scars aren't as noticeable. I do think that sometimes the transmasc community can have a problem with jealousy as it were, because dysphoria is not cute, and it can make you think and feel some not very nice things about yourself and other people. I remember being very jealous of people who got their top surgery before me, or they started T before I did, and I wonder if that's where it's coming from. People are projecting these feelings on to you, suggesting that you're not performing transness in the correct way.

CG: Yeah, I mean, I never would want to put words in anybody else's mouth, so I just leave it as it is. You know, everybody's surgery has had ups and downs and everything in between. Even though I may not have scars from a double mastectomy, I can still have my own feelings about my chest. Every time I see one of my nipples versus the other, I recall being in inpatient, literally digging at that damn thing when I wasn't supposed to be. *laughs* That's one of the reasons one of my nipples doesn't look the way the other one does, and even though I don't have the same scars as some other people, I still think about it! You don't think when I step out in broad daylight that I don't think, 'Well, there's that nipple that I took off.' *laughs*

But all I'm saying is people couldn't possibly know what you're experiencing. You don't owe an explanation to anybody, but false assumptions are exactly how we have problems, by making the wrong, inaccurate perception of somebody without even hearing what they have to say.

I had my surgery last April [2021], so very recently actually. And I think that by the time you take your shirt off for the first time, no one else is noticing any of the little things. But it's almost like a *hyper-awareness of your own body that you've never had before. I basically ignored my entire torso until I got top surgery *laughs*, so maybe there's this hyper-awareness of your own body all of a sudden.*

CG: Oh yeah, definitely. And also congratulations on that!

Thank you! I feel absolutely amazing. *laughs* I mentioned before, but when I was pre-T, I had this very rigid concept of what I would be like when I started hormones and I started passing as cis, and it was very stereotypically masculine. Oh yeah, I'm definitely going to join the gym, get ripped. *laughs* I did join the gym! I do enjoy working out a lot more than I did, but it's less of 'I have to do this to get stronger' and it's more about feeling the ways my body feels good now. Has your idea of masculinity changed over time?

CG: Yes, yes, yes, 100%. I think I was honestly just trying to – as a lot of us do – figure out who I actually am now that I know I'm a man. Do I like all these sports that I thought were only for guys? Do I like whatever hobby we assume is traditionally masculine? Do I like woodworking? I need to see who I am, now that I can finally say who I am. So I definitely dabbled and attempted to do so many things that I thought I might like if I gave it a chance. I can confidently say to this day that I ditched so many of those things. *laughs* But there are some things that now, in terms of masculinity, I just view as things I do that make me happy. I am too cheap to get my nails done, but if I had an expendable income and I wanted to go to a BIPOC- or even trans-run salon, I would 100% spend the money and get my nails done! If I had the time in my day to do makeup and it made me happy, then I would probably do that as well.

I am definitely one of those people that buys a lot of random things cheaply off the internet, and a lot of those would not abide by traditional standards of masculinity, but they make me very happy. So yeah, comfortable doing that. For me, masculinity and my own sense of masculinity is just doing what feels right for me. I always said this – I guess maybe later on in my transition than in the beginning – but I transitioned to be happy. I didn't transition to be viewed as a macho man, I didn't transition to be viewed as anything but me. I transitioned to make myself happy.

The thing about how I present myself and recently on a lot of my social media, I don't know what it's going to look like in the future. For example, I personally don't pack. I don't feel the need to at this time. Maybe I will, just to give it a shot as I do with multiple things, but for the sake of also providing other people with some type of person that they could relate to. It's kind of how I always envisioned masculinity prior to transitioning, and that makes me happy. And, you know, I'm sure there are plenty of people that are sitting at home going, 'Hm, there's a Speedo, but I'm pretty sure he's missing a pretty big component.' And the answer is, 'You know what? I'm not missing anything. I am living myself, in my body, the way I want it to look.'

I think that's an important point. A lot of growing into the man that you are is about realizing that masculinity is sometimes more about relaxing. *laughs* But these things you're interested in aren't necessarily masculine or feminine, as it were – they're more explorations of like, you as a person, right? And I think that's a lot of cisgender society placing these little boxes, and then engaging with the trans community more and talking to many people in the community is a

realization that there's so much more to our experiences than dyspho-
ria and passing. It's almost as though you can do any of these things,
and it's an exploration of your own potential – in a very flowery
*sentimental way of saying! *laughs**

CG: Yeah, I mean honestly that is such an accurate observation.
People don't realize that there's this huge intersectionality
between trans and gender-expansive culture and community,
and feminist activism. Because women who identify as women,
historically, obviously have had goals, ambitions, desires, hobbies
and the ability to do so many things that really have always been
reserved for men. So it's like now that we have this group of
individuals, the trans and gender-expansive community, saying
with honesty that we don't care what things are supposed to
be for, or who is in control of these rules. We pursue happiness.
You should fight and get the job that you deserve to get. You
should do the hobbies that make you happy. I can only speak
for myself, but I recall being that weird kid. *laughs* I was the
weird kid during lunch reading alien conspiracy books in the
library in fourth grade, reading about Bigfoot. I was trying to
talk to the boys about wrestling, and I did feel the sense of
shame. And I'm like, 'Why isn't anybody else doing this with
me?' It was literally me up there at the library reading about
Bigfoot, eating Lunchables, and all my friends who were girls
would be eating pudding and nice sandwiches downstairs and
like, talking about Barbie and stuff. And I remember asking
myself, 'Why isn't anybody else doing this?' And I kind of feel
like the trans and gender-expansive community, even as children
and adolescents, are showing we're doing what we're doing to
make us happy.

I definitely agree. I too was the weird kid in the library. *laughs* That's an interesting concept: shame. Asking yourself these questions and policing your own brain is a very important aspect of control over our actions. I do think it even impacts cisgender people, right? This inherent feeling that you shouldn't be doing this because you look or exist in a certain way and space.

CG: Oh yeah, that's the biggest part of it. It is a societal impact that is systemically placed upon a lot of transgender bodies.

I suppose that links back to this whole intersection of different identities, because it's almost that the way that people are allowed to explore and experiment is also incredibly tied up into class, for example, which you touched upon with regard to your own work. There is the privilege of being able to expand and perform, which is why something like your nonprofit is so important.

CG: Yeah 100%, which is why I think it's so important to be transparent. I'm benchmarking the pricing model of when we're actually able to get this thing up and running, I'm also very strongly utilizing the concept of mutual aid as well as an income-driven experience in order to serve the community, which does look like a lot of shared resources. It'll be an income-driven model, so people will have a very safe, non-invasive way of being able to supply this additional background information so that they can have access to the same high-quality resources as those who are able to pay the actual entry fee to get in.

That sounds incredible. I think that's one of the things I value so much about the trans community, and the queer community as a whole, but it's something I find specifically in a lot of trans spaces – this core focus of mutual aid. I've been to a lot of events that are 'pay what you can', and we've always been very ready to share resources and information regarding transition, as well as wider projects. The sense of community is so strong and it is so built upon. We are in this very unique space where we have almost built our own model of mutual aid and support, often for our own survival, which I think is a really important and valuable thing to platform.

CG: Yes, which makes things better for everybody.

What is something that you love?

CG: Ah, in what way?

laughs Whatever way you want. I will throw that your way and you can hit me with something.

CG: I mean, there are so many things in life that I find such strong passions for! I would say I love knowing that my intentions are matching my actions. I feel like there are so many times when our actions may be mistaken for other intentions, or intentions may be mistaken by our actions. So when I'm able to thoroughly express through my actions, through my choice of words, what I actually mean, I get a lot of fulfillment.

That really extends to everything in my life. From me intending to do something different in the gym and three weeks from then I did exactly what I intended to do, perfect. If that means intending to have my dog be happier by taking longer walks, perfect! I would just say actually being able to see the product of what I put in the work for brings me a lot of happiness. If that's how I'm doing at school, if that's doing volunteer work. This is just a silly example, but my friend's boyfriend and I handed out literature during the election, and, as we had hoped, we didn't have the same results as we had the election prior! We had a change of administration, so we work towards that baby step in terms of the guidelines of America, to making our community better. Obviously, it's just a chip of a step in the right direction, but it felt good to know we contributed to the results of the election and that is exactly what happened. We worked for it and there it was. That makes me happy.

I like that! Sometimes it's easy to forget that it does feel good to have your efforts recognized, even if you're just recognizing them yourself. I think it's easy to get lost in this big picture, or 'Why haven't I changed the entire world?' So I like that you appreciate and take the time to recognize yourself.

CG: Yeah, definitely.

Is there anything else you would like to add?

CG: I would just say, to kind of sum it all up, what I tell everybody. I just always, always, always tell everybody – we talked about the assumption thing already, but I cannot stress this enough – whatever journey someone is taking, the biggest act of self-love is never comparing your own. Your personal experience is such a private, beautiful thing, you know, and focusing on that act of self-appreciation is important regardless of whatever anybody else's process is in life. Do not compare yourself to anybody.

It's never about who is further along, or who is getting higher up the ladder in work or school. It's about being who you are and being who you want to be in a way that always radiates that you're going to be happier in the future, and that you're taking steps to make sure that your own protection of your mental health wellbeing is coming number one.

Fox Fisher

Fox Fisher (he/they) is a brown, queer, transmasculine, non-binary artist, author, filmmaker and LGBTQIA+ rights advocate. Fox co-founded and runs the My Genderation project, creating 100+ short films. In 2018, Fox was awarded an honorary doctorate for their work on trans issues in film and the media. Fox is a patron for LGBT Switchboard, co-founder and trustee of Trans Pride (Brighton), advisor to All About Trans and was artist in residence for Homotopia Festival in late 2020. They made art for the Tate's Queer & Now exhibition in 2021. Fox's books include *Trans Pride: A Coloring Book, Trans Teen Survival Guide, Trans Survival Workbook* and a gentle gender-nonconforming kid's book, *Are You a Boy or Are You a Girl?*

How long have you been making films?

FF: I've been making films as a form of activism for the past nine years, after coming out as trans and taking part in a mainstream documentary series called *My Transsexual Summer*, which followed seven trans people's lives and put us in a house together.

The documentary was an 'observational one' (which doesn't necessarily mean factual), had a massive budget, was on prime-time television and started a conversation with the nation on trans issues. Unfortunately, despite four one-hour episodes, the team failed to tell my story sensitively, creating their own narrative about me struggling as an artist (which never made the edit), when the real story was about my family getting used to me coming out, my struggle with waiting times, self-medicating and desperately wanting top surgery.

The series was made by an entirely non-trans production company, so after the series was aired to a massive audience, I teamed up with another participant, Lewis Hancox, bought a second-hand camera from a guy at a Burger King at King's Cross in London and started making films about trans people around me. This was my therapy. Filmmaking is an incredibly powerful medium and very addictive.

Having started out making cut-and-paste zines, I am comfortable in the counterculture, where it feels more real, raw, and can often influence the mainstream.

I agree! Is it frustrating to compare your experiences on such a high-budget set (where your experiences were constructed for an audience) to how you create art now?

FF: Definitely – it's mainly sad to see that production companies and terrestrial channels don't see the benefit of having trans people create content about trans people, as it is always going to end up being a more authentic representation. But I guess that goes to show that the big media platforms don't necessarily want that – they want something that sells, something that is made by them, for them, even if it's to the detriment of transgender people. I just think that's profoundly sad.

Did you always want to explore transness in film, or did that develop alongside other activism?

FF: My focus, since coming out, has been to show the world that trans people are just people. I think this will always be my focus. However, when I first started filmmaking, there was a lack of documentaries about trans lives, which has changed a lot over the years. Film is such a powerful medium and quite addictive. There are many people who might not read an article but can be reached through film, online or on the big screen. Now, my interest is much more in fiction, historical storytelling, music videos and experimental arty film.

To me, filmmaking is just a branch of my trans advocacy, equally important as books, articles, podcasts, consultancy or even fashion shows, which reflect that trans people are just people.

I do think there is such a power in incorporating our experiences into fiction and other forms of art. I suppose it counters this misconception that documentary is the only way of exploring something 'factually' or 'authentically', but actually if we're only shown as a subject, it has the potential to be quite othering.

I think we definitely need to start seeing more than just documentaries about trans people. Fiction has a powerful way of showing people's humanity in a different way – this has worked really well for people of underrepresented groups, especially when it's on more high-profile TV shows or series where they do it well.

How important is it to you that we, as trans people, get to tell our own stories?

FF: It's critical for trans people to be able to share our stories. This is why I'm obsessed with helping to raise the platform of older trans people, through the story of *Inverness or Bust*, which we are starting to film and have fundraised enough to buy the equipment we need to do it justice. The stories of older trans people often die out when they pass away, and it's so important for us to honour our trans elders and understand what they had to go through in order to be themselves.

Inverness or Bust is a historical documentary that tells the tale of a fateful road trip that a group of trans people went on in 1975. At the time, the term 'transgender' hadn't even been coined and trans people faced an incredible amount of stigma and discrimination. Getting medical treatment was very difficult, but a few trans people caught wind that a surgeon up in Inverness in Scotland was willing to talk to them about medical treatment. So they took to the road.

In this documentary, Carol, Nemo and Stephen – core members of the original group – will travel with a group of younger trans people the same route that they went back in the day, reminiscing about this fateful journey. On the way, they will meet up with young trans people across the UK. This will allow a cross-generational conversation between trans people, while offering us valuable insight into trans history and how things were, how things are now and where we still need to go.[1]

Does the way you've had to present yourself in the past differ from your actual lived experiences?

FF: You cannot judge a book by its cover. In the past, when my presentation didn't match how I felt, then people didn't relate to me in a way that felt affirming. I have a different issue now, where my presentation doesn't reflect all my years accessing women's spaces, being part of the queer scene.

I had to relinquish access to women's spaces where I felt more comfortable, and it's not like I want to be part of all-male groups. I feel that non-binary people, like myself, can feel quite isolated.

That's a very interesting point! So, for you, does it feel as though you've had to give up an aspect of yourself or your personal history in order to be respected?

FF: I just feel like the idea of these spaces is incredibly binary and restricting for all of us. Yes, there are spaces that people need where they can feel safer, from cis men in particular – but anyone who isn't a cis man needs that. It's just frustrating that I never truly fit into any space, and I certainly don't feel comfortable in a room or a space full of cis men.

---

1   My Genderation (n.d.) *'Inverness or Bust* Press Release.' Accessed on 13/01/2022 at https://docs.google.com/document/d/1znLkJXMj5puOvWj5Z1xNV uxetJoKIecTwpGPffl8HWw/edit.

Is there a way we can better support our non-binary siblings from within the trans community?

FF: I think that within the trans community itself, we need to be aware of different identities and people, and how their experiences can intersect. My experiences, for example, greatly align with the experiences of trans men – because of my expression, my hormones, the surgeries I've had and so on. So we need to be able to move beyond these binary categories altogether.

How has being so much in the public eye with your identity affected how you interact with yourself and other people?

FF: I didn't ever think I'd be so involved in helping to educate on trans issues and fight in the trenches, so I must be careful about how it can overwhelm me, because it's such a heart-wrenching situation. A lot of my work cannot be done on an individual basis, although I always try to respond to someone reaching out and send them to what I hope will be better support for them, locally and nationally.

There are things I can change and those I can light a candle for and send love to. This ranges from trans children being removed from loving parents, to older trans people still traumatized from their treatment over the years, and worse. The other day I accidentally saw a film of such unspeakable torture of a trans woman that I can only wish that she has now passed to end her pain. Our government not only needs to be supporting trans people in the UK, which they are completely failing to do, but should also be putting pressure on other countries to uphold basic human rights.

I feel that any sort of platform online I have is small in comparison to others who might be known for being a trans actor, musician or model. I try to use what I have to raise awareness of trans issues; however, it can feel very frustrating.

On a daily basis, I get nasty comments online, and much of my time is spent reporting, deleting and blocking online. Once or twice a year, I might be asked to speak on national radio or TV, and often I refuse because I know the host is unsympathetic to trans issues or I am being pitted against a transphobe. It is incredibly frustrating and sometimes I wonder what I might have achieved over the past ten years if I wasn't busy defending my right to exist and putting out fires caused by fear-mongering in the mainstream media.

Doing an interview, like the one on live breakfast TV with Piers Morgan, brought mountains of abuse before, during and after the interview. I started recognizing burnout and anxiety associated with speaking out. My partner and I have been featured in articles that have been shared over and over again by people telling us to kill ourselves or calling us slurs. It's exhausting.

So what needs to change in how we're represented on screen?

FF: The narrative that's being created in the media in regard to 'the trans debate' is often the complete opposite of the reality of things. Trans people suffer great amounts of abuse and harassment for advocating for their rights every single day, both on social media and in their real life. Personally, I receive abusive comments on social media every single day, ranging from offensive name-calling to transphobic statements to death threats and serious abuse. This is simply for advocating for a more fair and just world, where trans people are treated with dignity and respect. Logging on to social media has become exhausting, and having to rifle through abusive comments to block and delete endless sock puppet accounts is incredibly taxing on me.

We have research after research after research telling us how badly trans people are treated in the UK and beyond, such as hate crimes against trans people having quadrupled in the UK in the last five years,[2] with over 65% of trans people hiding their identities at work[3] out of fear of discrimination, and reports of high suicide rates and extreme violence across the world. Trans people are being painted as the aggressors, when in fact we have never faced more extreme prejudice, discrimination and violence. It is clear the media has a far-right agenda to push, and trans people are the target. That's the root of all of these 'arguments' and 'concerns', and it's really sad to see people falling prey to it so easily.

The media constantly gives a platform to stories or narratives that have little place in reality or factual evidence behind them. Anyone who has a negative opinion of trans people has suddenly become an expert on trans issues, without having any expertise, experience or relevance to the topic at hand. Most people who are speaking out against trans rights have never even had a real

2   Chapple, T. (2020) 'Hate crimes against trans people have quadrupled in the last five years', BBC News, 11 October. Accessed on 13/01/2022 at www.bbc.co.uk/news/av/uk-54486122.

3   '"Trans employee experiences survey: Understanding the trans community in the workplace" (2021) – research conducted by Totaljobs.' Accessed on 13/01/2022 at www.totaljobs.com/advice/trans-employee-experiences-survey-2021-research-conducted-by-totaljobs.

conversation with a trans person or spent any valuable time getting to know the community or the issues we face. How can someone be seen as qualified to talk about a topic without any relevance to it?

Obviously, there are a lot of negatives that come with being publicly out as trans, but how has it impacted your life positively?

FF: Personally, it's been a wonderful opportunity to connect with real people who are as passionate as I am when it comes to trans rights and being treated as a human being. Without being known for making films, I wouldn't have found love with my non-binary trans partner Ugla (Owl) or had the opportunity to travel to Russia and other Pride events globally.

By being out as trans, I've been able to take on trans-specific work, like the series of films I was commissioned to make at TGEU (Trans Europe), which is where I met my partner Owl. My partner being trans is a huge comfort to me. We understand each other on a deep level.

Being trans has been entwined in my advancement as a film-maker, author and artist. I've been to fancy parties at the Gherkin for Channel 4, had my own events at Channel 4, YouTube Pride parties and been invited to 10 Downing Street three times in the past ten years.

Through All About Trans, I've been able to chat with top gatekeepers in print and broadcast on trans issues. I've consulted on trans storylines in *Hollyoaks*, *EastEnders*, *Emmerdale*, Netflix shows and more.

It must be so empowering to interact with so many in the community!

Does it also feel good to interact with so many allies and cis people who work alongside you to give you the space to tell our stories?

FF: We really need our allies to make progress – so I am always really happy to work with allies and cis people in general who are willing to help combat transphobia. They can access spaces and situations that trans people can't, and they often have the power to sway others in a way that we don't, so I think the more allies we can get on board, the better.

Was there ever a point in your life when you did believe that the expected presentation was how you would have to learn to accept yourself? In other words, did you ever feel pressure to be 'binary'?

FF: The issue I had with *My Transsexual Summer* (Channel 4) ten years ago was not being able to be out as non-binary. I identified as genderqueer at the time and was told to simplify my experience because 'the Channel 4 audience wouldn't understand'. It was the same language that I had to use for my GP and the GIC when accessing healthcare, parroting statements like 'I should have been born a boy' and 'I feel like a man'. This felt incredibly frustrating – that I wasn't fully 'seen' and I was having to conform despite having pushed through the first hurdle of coming out as trans and starting to change my whole life. With the effects of hormones and top surgery, I am 'on the surface' read as a cis man, which means the world doesn't fully see me, but it's better than being read as a woman, which I was not. For safety, this helps, although I am still subjected to homophobic abuse as I'm not always read as a heterosexual. I don't like football or all-male spaces, so I still feel like an outsider. Gym changing rooms still give me anxiety and I try to change my clothes as quickly as possible in spaces like that.

Did it take some time to discover how masculinity fit into your identity and worldview? Do/did you ever feel at odds with masculinity?

FF: Yes! Having had the experience of many men in my life being sexist, dominating a space and sometimes being violent abusers, I lacked decent male role models.

I felt deeply connected with femmes, knowing the difficulties and dangers femmes face, although I often felt like an imposter as one. There was a lot to unpack.

How did you begin to conceptualize masculinity as something other than a destructive force?

FF: Kicking a ball around, climbing trees, making forts, riding a BMX were unusual for a girl to do, but not entirely denied to me, so that was never really reserved for boys or exclusively masculine. It was clothing for special occasions or the swimming pool that I really struggled with, perhaps because it always gendered me as female. When I was able to wear a T-shirt and shorts, I'd often be mistaken for a boy, especially when my hair was cut short, and wonky, by my own hands. As I hit 11 or 12 years old, things felt off for me. I had a fear of puberty and that I'd feel even more disconnected, which turned out to be true. I struggled to connect with being a woman, and I couldn't find much connection in conventionally alpha-macho manly men's men. I began to notice all the positive masculine people in my life, sensitive men like Kurt Cobain or Samir, a quiet and beautiful boy in my school. I realized the fragility of the construct of gender, the mask of masculinity, because men and boys were put under enormous pressure to be aggressive, warfaring, repress emotions, not cry, etc.

Do you think being non-binary has helped explore those concepts in more depth?

FF: I think visibility for non-binary people is really making us think about what we mean when we say 'man' and 'woman' – identity is so much more complex than we in the West have ever really considered.

Do you think being extra aware of those nuances in yourself helped identify what parts of masculinity were possibly less beneficial to you and those around you?

FF: Being aware that I was more than my gender helped me to recognize that my identity existed beyond the construct, in a spiritual way.

I've noticed that your art, especially the stuff you do with My Genderation, is focused mostly on exploring and expressing trans experiences at our happiest – the support we get, how those you film have found themselves. Why is that the image you want to promote above all else?

FF: We aren't afraid to go to dark places with stories in My Genderation films; however, 'overcoming obstacles' is our key phrase. With so many negative and false portrayals of trans people in the media, it's important to have films that show light at the end of the tunnel. We deserve that sort of narrative and yet still honour the struggle.

Do you have a favourite My Genderation project?

FF: *Get Off My Turf!* was a great film to work on, because it's fictional and we were able to utilize what was around us to make it. Locations are simple, including my own home, my neighbour's garden and the green area overlooking my garden. The tree in my back garden blossoms for about two weeks of the year, and when it started to bloom, I knew we had a very short window to film the garden scenes. I've definitely gravitated towards more fiction. It's all storytelling, but there's more opportunity for poetry and creative licenses with fiction.

What would seeing images like that onscreen have done for you as a younger person?

FF: Having been able to see myself reflected back, as a young transmasculine kid, would have helped me to realize what was possible, helping me to feel more connected with who I was, less of an outsider missing a puzzle piece.

Instead, I connected with coming-of-age boy films like *Oliver Twist*, *Power of One*, *Flight of the Navigator* and *Stand by Me*.

What's it like working with an all-trans team?

FF: For creating trans content, it's everything to have an all-trans team. This is so important to me, to cut out any cis filter. By that, I mean that cis people often have a specific focus on hormones and surgeries for a trans person and might not realize certain clichés they are reinforcing with camera shots of a trans woman putting on her makeup or a trans man binding with ACE bandages. Working with trans people cuts out that cis-spective, which helps relax the person being filmed, thus creating more intimate and authentic content. I learned this the hard way, having dealt with what I now consider PTSD [post-traumatic stress disorder] after being filmed and edited by an entirely cis crew for the *My Transsexual Summer* series on C4 in 2011.

What is something you wish people knew about you?

FF: I'm a POC [person of colour]. I'm sensitive. I have lost many, many people in my life, all LGBTQIA+, which leaves a gaping hole that's impossible to fill. I'm spiritual although not religious.

Charlie Caine

Charlie (he/him) is a theatre director and composer from the UK. He describes himself as a socialist campaigner and believes strongly in the power of direct action and mutual aid. Currently, he is working on a theatre piece about the trans experience, hoping to explore our struggles and joys on the stage.

So first of all, would you like to introduce yourself?

CC: Yeah, sure, absolutely! I'm Charlie Caine, pronouns he/him. I call myself a queer theatre-maker, which, I would say, means that I'm queer, and I make theatre, and I make queer theatre. I'm mostly a composer, lyricist and poet, and I also work a little bit as a performer and musical director.

How long have you been writing, and have you always been involved in theatre specifically?

CC: I've been involved in theatre since I was a kid. I have a very strong memory of when I was seven, going into the living room and announcing to my parents: 'I'm going to be an actor.' *laughs* And they were great! They signed me up for drama classes. It was very lucky in those days. We weren't a wealthy family at all; I come from a working-class family and grew up in one of the poorest council estates in Norwich. But some things were easier then. This was in the 1990s, so things were a lot easier then, and they signed me up for some great drama classes at the Theatre Royal in Norwich, which I did right through until I was 18. It was a great youth theatre there.

In terms of writing, it was when I was about 11. Funnily enough, the company I was involved in, their adult and older youth did a production of *Into the Woods*, which is a Stephen Sondheim musical, and that was the thing for me. I'd done little bits of creative writing before, but that was the thing for me that I suddenly went, 'Wow, no, this is what I really want to do.'

I wanted to be able to write that kind of stuff and have other people perform it. It was a magical experience for me, and I've been writing since then.

Is that what attracts you to theatre as a medium? Seeing your own creations performed on the stage?

CC: That's definitely one of the things. I'd say as a performer, what I used to love about it was the escape, and it was the same thing with the piano for me. So I played the piano – I started the piano at the age of five, so that was even earlier, and those were all great creative outlets for me to just escape from life, you know, and particularly with the theatre and linking it to transness, you can become someone completely different, you know. When you do theatre – at any age, but especially as a kid – you will always find there is a gender imbalance. There are far less boys than there are girls. What that meant was that I was always cast in boys' roles, which was a real gender-affirming thing for me to do. I could escape into this character and become this person.

In terms of the writing, there is something very special about knowing – I suppose this may be a bit egotistical – that I created this. This piece started out as nothing. It was just an idea in my head, and I created it, and now other people are performing it and other people are watching, and it's become this tangible thing.

I don't know how related it is to this, but I think for me as a young person, I knew quite early on that I was trans and I was going to transition. I accepted very early on that I'm never going to have children, and writing becomes almost like a child. *laughs* This is your baby. This is the thing you have created and it's very precious to you.

*One of my most vivid early trans memories is being in middle school, and we did a production of Romeo and Juliet. The teachers told us we could write down if we would mind being cast in a male or female role. And I didn't know what the feeling was, but I was so excited! *laughs* Almost like playing a different part is a way, even when you don't have the language for it, of navigating some quite complex feelings that you just don't have the words for when you're younger.*

CC: Yes, absolutely. I mean, we're performing gender all the time anyway, and you know, obviously cis people are performing in the same way, but when you're acting, you're getting a lot of practice at performing gender and performing different variations of it. So, for example, I remember one of the parts I was cast in when I was young was this school bully, who was someone who was being beaten up by his dad, and so he had a lot of trauma that he took out on other people. Now, I was never a bully as a child. But I was performing this toxic masculinity, and so it's interesting that it gives you all those different opportunities to perform gender in a different way. Certainly, the company I went to, they were a really, really top-notch theatre company. A lot of people have gone on from that company to being professional actors and working in the theatre. We've even got a few film stars who used to be in there. So we got proper theatre training from a young age, so when we had a character, we would be asked to really envelop their character and come up with backstories for them, and live their lives. It was all giving me real gender euphoria, I suppose.

Have you found it easy to exist as a trans person in that space?

CC: On a personal level, I have been fairly lucky. Being in the theatre as a kid, you grow up around queer people. I mean, the theatre is incredibly gay, mainly cis gay men, but you just grow up around it. I think there are at least two other people who were in the arts course at different times to me who have also transitioned. I think it is something that trans kids get attracted to as well, and so I definitely got used to being in queer spaces. As we mentioned, the casting really helped me – that was very affirming. I do know others who have had problems. You know, the theatre, like any other institution, has issues with systemic racism and transphobia – even homophobia – and almost the higher up you get, the more intense that becomes.

A lot of my life, until 2015, I was living stealth. So I was just kind of going into rehearsals and things as a guy, assumed to be cis. I never really had to deal with transphobia because no one knew. It wasn't until I recognized that it was going to be a political fight that I realized that I had to stand up. So, personal level, I can't really say anything that I have found specifically difficult about being in the theatre that wouldn't just be how it is difficult to exist as a trans person anyway.

The concept of being stealth is something that I think about a lot, actually. I've been on testosterone for long enough that I pass pretty much all the time now. For a long time, though, being stealth was never really an opportunity for me. It feels really good to just be able to relax and just exist. It is nice to walk into a space and be just a guy, but then it is this internal conflict. This is a political fight. People seeing me and me being seen by other people is something that is becoming increasingly important.

CC: Absolutely, and one of the things that I felt for me was important specifically as a trans man to do that was because we disrupt the classic transphobic narratives that focus on and demonize trans women. I also think that you do get a degree of male privilege. When you speak as a man, your voice is listened to more, and so I do feel a kind of level of responsibility there to be one of the people that stands up and is vocal and is seen.

Do you ever feel pressured to tone yourself down for an audience?

CC: Yeah, it's an interesting one. I mean, no, I don't think I ever have for an audience if I'm honest. Certainly, in real life, but not when I'm on stage. I suppose, if anything, I tone up. When you're creating something dramatic, you want it to be more – you want it to be bigger. When I do the performance of 'Transphobia: A Plea to the Media' for my show – or when I will be doing it – I strip. Generally, I don't read angry poems nude. *laughs* I'd say, in life, what I've found really interesting and one of the things that I think is nicest about transitioning is that I can act much more naturally than before. I think this is the case for a lot of trans men. In the beginning, it's kind of about toning down, you know – like don't talk too much with your hands, sit in a specific position, don't sit with your legs crossed. Don't wear bright colours, don't have long hair – it's all these rules. One thing I found very freeing about transition, and I think it's the case for a lot of guys, is that actually once you are being seen as a man by cis people, you are freer, in your personal life at least, to be more expressive, to be camper, to be more feminine. All the things that you're suppressing, you can suddenly let loose, and that's more me.

I would identify as a gay man and quite camp. I don't think of myself as particularly macho, and the men I grew up around in the theatre, they were all very expressive. So my view of masculinity from a young age was shaped by that.

So I'd say I've toned down in life before I transitioned, but once I had, I think there are more and more things that I feel freer to do and freer to express myself in certain ways.

I definitely have that same experience, because I used to think that I would need to flatten myself out and show as few emotions as possible. But again that just makes you very miserable. And I do think the *concept of passing privilege is weird, and again a very complex issue. But it is the ability and the freedom to be more expressive and you are able to act more naturally. You can't see me on camera, but I'm gesturing a lot! *laughs**

CC: Yes! *laughs* It's funny because there is a thing around invisibility. Trans men – we are invisible. There's also a thing of passing through the world as a man – you are invisible. I transitioned fairly young, as a teenager. I don't have the experience that some trans guys have of having to walk out in the world being seen as women, you know, but I am still very well aware of the fact that women get hassled on the street. When I have women friends talk to me about the kind of stuff that they have to put up with on a daily basis, and it's like, well, I just exist. I walk outside my house and I exist outside my house, and that's the way it is.

Yeah, that is interesting. I talk about this with some of the other guys that I've spoken to. The invisibility we experience has led to a significant disregard for our rights and the issues we face but is also a privilege in its own way. That is something that is quite difficult to navigate, in terms of where we fit into the conversations that are being had.

CC: Absolutely, yes.

Were you ever worried that producing certain works or acting a certain way would make people take you less seriously?

CC: I don't think I have been, honestly. I was lucky in a lot of ways. You know, it all goes back to growing up around the theatre, growing up around people that are different. Those expectations even of masculinity are different in those groups, and so I don't think I really ever have felt that, in terms of theatre. Though I would say, it's only recently that I've started to bring gender into theatre.

When you're a composer, lyricist, generally you're an interpreter, yeah? So a playwright will write the book and it is their work – essentially, it's coming from them. Obviously, the songs come from me, but it's coming from their perspective. It's something they're passionate about or want to write, and you are interpreting their story. So I think one of the things that is interesting about the piece that I'm writing at the moment is that it's the first time I've written something which is me, so it is my story. I'm not interpreting someone else.

Because of the nature of the piece, I don't think that no one will take it seriously. I want people to go out, I want cis people to go out feeling quite shocked and educated. There is a great deal of trans liberation as part of it as well, because I want trans people to go out feeling joyful.

It's interesting you say about taking seriously, because this just sprung to my mind, which is when you think about queer theatre or queer media in general, a big central tenet of that is trauma. In order to tell this story of what's happening to us now, and what's happened to us in the past, that trauma has got to be a part of it, but it is so rare that we actually concentrate on queer joy. I think it's really important, and that's really important for the community that actually, no matter how cis people come out feeling, trans people come out feeling and know that we've got a lot of strength, and there is a lot of joy in our experience.

Trans joy is something that isn't focused on in any kind of media. I do think that one of the reasons young trans people struggle a lot is because all they have when they try to see themselves is suffering.

CC: Yeah, I think the one thing that I would say is that, again, it does have trauma as well. I think *Pose* has done a lot of good work there. I've spent a lot of time watching the last season that came out recently. I just remember watching it and thinking that this is the first time that I can remember seeing something that was specifically written for me, you know. If a cisgender heterosexual person watches it, they're probably going to enjoy it, but they're not going to get it on that visceral level. All the stuff around AIDS is quite traumatic, and poverty, all of that. Obviously, it's because that's the reality of our lives, you know. Unless you're doing a fantastical piece, you've got to show reality. But there was also a huge amount of joy.

Actually, I do think that what is missing from a lot of cis-centric narratives in any media is just love as a concept in general. Even when things are sad, which is obviously an important part of our reality, but love is the experience. My trans experience is centred so much around love for the community and myself. I think if I walked out of a theatre and felt as though that has been noted and feel that that is recognized, that would have done something incredible for me when I started transitioning.

CC: Yeah, absolutely! It's funny, that is something that does totally get missed. There's this transphobic narrative that if we transition, this is going to be so hard and you're going to find this so hard, and you'll find it very difficult to have a relationship.

I've had multiple relationships! Any difficulty I've had has been my own internalized shame. On a personal level, I've never found that there's a difficulty there other than that I've put on myself.

I remember seeing this sexual health charity put out something about gay trans men, specifically for gay men, I think. Again, it was going into how you might find it hard to have relationships and all this. It was like, 'Why are you trying to make it sound so utterly miserable?' Also, just on an objective level, trans people are hot. *laughs*

*Exactly! *laughs* I have never found it difficult to be desired, actually.*

CC: A lot of that comes from the things we see in our media. I mean, I grew up in the era of *Ace Ventura*, which I think was the film that really brought in the trope of someone sleeping with a trans woman and vomiting. So throughout your upbringing, you're told you are unlovable. Whether you have sex with people or not, or have relationships. Obviously, that's a bonus as far as I'm concerned, but that's not the reason to transition or not.

But then through the GIC as well, you have this perception of us. When I was transitioning, it was even worse. Fortunately, I was able to go private for my first assessments and stuff, because it wasn't as expensive as it is now. So I was privileged enough to be able to skip all of that, but I remember the reason I decided to skip it was because of talking to other gay trans men and them saying, 'Do not tell them you are gay. Because they want you to be more normal, and so if you're transitioning you'll become straight, and therefore you are somehow more "normal".' To be gay would be less normal.

That's awful! I don't think it's as bad as it was – I was able to talk about my boyfriend with my clinician, when I was still with him. I do still kind of 'de-camp' myself when I go to the GIC, though. I will wear a hoodie and jeans, and maybe a pair of trainers. Just because you want to be the least gender-nonconforming as possible, in case they don't believe you. I don't know if it's necessary anymore, but I've always done it, and I know people who will or continue to always do it, and whenever they go, I think that's just something we're going to be paranoid about.

CC: Yes, it is ridiculous. Also, we have all this scare around detransitioning – what if someone gets it wrong? Well, you know, if you create a system where people don't think they have to lie in order to get medication, then you're less likely to get people who have regrets later on. Obviously, 'regrets' isn't a reason to withhold healthcare, but just to kind of use that narrative so it's often thrown around.

Do you think being trans enriches your creative work?

CC: Yes, 100%. I mean, it enriches my life as well and it's something I try to remind myself of daily. There's a great quote from Hannah Gadsby's *Nanette* where she talks about shame. She says, you know, 'I know up here. I've intellectualized it and I know that there's nothing wrong with me, but it's still there.' I can definitely relate to that. It's certainly a lot better than it used to be, but you grow up being told you are wrong and unlovable, seeing all these different things thrown at you. It's very difficult to get rid of that. And I think it's really important to think about how, as queer people in general and definitely as trans people, we are going to have an outlook on gender and on life that cis people just can't. I think it does bring a more colourful perspective. It gives you a more full perspective of the world, so I try to remind myself that, actually, I'm grateful for that and I'm grateful as a creative person every single day.

In terms of how it has affected my creative writing? Well, I don't think I would be a writer. Well, I don't know – it's hard to say. But I'm pretty certain that what I mean by that is that me creating started as a means of escape, and a means to escape fear. I had other childhood trauma and difficulties as well, from some family difficulties that I won't go into, but I needed to escape. So I created these worlds from a very young age. I was just creating worlds which I would go into. That kind of doesn't stop – that's what being a writer is. I always think that, as a writer, you've got to maintain some of that childish nature. Some of that stuff that you have from a very young age, that sense of 'I'm going to do this mad thing that an adult would say is ridiculous.'

In terms of how it influences what I write now, I'm obviously writing a piece around gender, and this is the first full piece I'm doing around that. This is the first piece that was really based around transphobia trends, being trans in society and trans liberation. I think I've noticed more these days that there's a real push for people to be telling their stories. Generally, if you want to tell a story about trans people, people will generally prefer you get a trans person to write it and to perform it. These arguments come around all the time about whether artists should be able to create what they like. I don't care what the rights and wrongs are as an artist. It is your job to evolve with society. If you can't, your art dies. So, at the moment, it is very big for us to really look at identities and to have people who have those identities exploring them, so that's what I'm doing. If in five years' time that changes, well, I'll change with it.

So, yeah, I mean in that respect, obviously when I'm writing about what's happening, I have experienced it personally, I feel it personally. I know the anger. I feel the anger, and so when I write it into those poems or those songs, it is a very, very personal experience. It's not one step removed, and I think that only makes it stronger.

That makes a lot of sense, especially because, as you were saying, it is about people feeling seen.

CC: No, absolutely, and that's what I would say this piece at the moment is about. I'm writing it for trans people. I want us to be my core audience. I'd love for cis people to come and to be somewhat educated by it, but they're not who it is specifically for. It's so rare that stuff is specifically written about us in a way that a cisgender person could enjoy, but I want to feel seen by it.

In a society and media sphere where we are feeling increasingly invisible, invisible in terms of how we are unable to construct our own narratives and the reality of our narratives, I think that's so important.

CC: When we think about bigotries and prejudice, at a fundamental level they're systemic things, and we all grow up with them. We internalize them. We either internalized them as a member of that group or we internalize them as not a member of that group, so, if you want to be a decent person, your job is to try to break those things down. In terms of trans people, at the moment we are being spoken about in the most monstrous way. And so it becomes normalized to use hate speech. Any cis creators who are trying to write trans characters can get it so wrong because they forget that you've got to do your research and treat us as human beings. You can't take what's being spread about us at face value. I think because we have been so dehumanized for so long and so visibly, at the moment it's very easy for a cis creator to forget that.

I don't really have a problem with cis people writing about us, but if you're going to, at least talk to us and at least listen to us, because sometimes they do talk, but generally they talk at us. It's not listening.

I saw you at the Trans Rights Protest where you performed 'Transphobia: A Plea to the Media' and it is a piece that resonated and affected everyone there, as it was supposed to. I was struck by this very clear anger throughout, and I was wondering if you found yourself harnessing those feelings in your work in the arts and also elsewhere.

CC: Yes, definitely. And creativity has always been a big way for me to harness it from quite a young age. There's creative anger, and anger at life. In terms of creatively, I've been quite lucky in that I have always been able to harness anger and I've used it, so if I've ever had someone tell me I'm going to fail, it's always been a drive to prove them wrong. I've always been quite good at that. Obviously, lots of things make me angry in the news at the moment, but if I think about it creatively: 'OK, this is something I can harness.'

I mean a lot of anger was brought into that poem. I'm sure you can absolutely tell, so I'm 100% harnessing it and using it in creativity. And it is something that I would definitely recommend other people do.

Pre-transition, I found it difficult to understand emotions as healthy or natural, because I did think I just wasn't supposed to have any, and so anger for me was always inherently destructive and there was no way to use it as a constructive force. How have you found the difference between destructive and constructive anger? Is there a difference, and how do you navigate that?

CC: Another way for me, by the way, is playing the piano. *laughs* I have a specific piece of music that I will hammer out on the piano when I'm angry.

I did a lot of thinking around this actually, because, funnily enough, I have other issues around here, and it's weird because in my brain I had never really linked it to being trans. Growing up, I had my dad, who never displayed any anger even when it would have been justified, and my mum, who was quite quick to anger. I had these two polar opposites of anger in my life, and the one I would always try to veer towards was my dad's side anyway. I think it just gave me, growing up and even now as an adult, this feeling of not knowing when it is appropriate to display anger, and how it is appropriate to display anger. I think that's probably helped creatively, because I do know it's appropriate to display anger there.

I would say, as a teenager, I kind of became a little bit misogynistic, so I definitely got a little bit of toxic masculinity mixed up with it as well. I worked that out of myself fairly quickly, but I think I was trying too hard. It's interesting because it's probably almost exactly the same for cis men, you know. When you take on those toxic views, it's because you are telling yourself this is how you are a man, and so you have to kind of unlearn.

In terms of how I try to frame it to myself now, I try to remind myself that actually anger is never inappropriate. It is never inappropriate to feel anger, even if it's not really the emotion you're feeling. Or the thing you're feeling anger towards. You're thinking, 'Well, this is a silly thing to feel anger towards.' I get angry with myself because I'm always losing things. You have to reframe it: you just lose the car keys a lot, but it's not the worst failing of a human being. The way you feel is never inappropriate. It's about how you express that. I think for me, where it still becomes difficult is where it's around confrontation. A lot of people don't like confrontation. But there are times where it is appropriate in a professional and personal context, times where it is appropriate and right to stand up for yourself. It's about knowing that, 'OK, I feel this, what do I do with it now?'

Absolutely harness it creatively. Absolutely harness it for protest. But if it's something in my personal life, I just sit with it. I'm right to feel angry. You cannot help your feelings. They are natural reactions, and you are always right to feel them.

I do think anger is a very complicated concept for trans men. It's almost as though we're not supposed to take up space and have these feelings because we're 'women', and then suddenly as soon as you start passing as a man, it's toxic masculinity and it's suddenly this destructive force.

CC: Yeah, absolutely. Thinking of it in political terms as well, because we are so invisible politically, our anger often gets put on hold. For example, I'm really angry at the moment that there are no bottom surgeons in the UK right now. I feel like that's not given a voice, because it's at the bottom of a long list of things. We're so constantly fighting to change the narrative, there's no space for us to speak about our real injustices and experiences.

What do you think is missing from the current discussions we're having in transmasculine spaces?

CC: I think what we really need to be doing is focusing on our liberation, which we're not doing at the moment because we're focusing on fighting. People come at us with an attack and we fight that attack, and we're having to just keep fighting. I think we need to be bringing back direct action groups. I want to see us out there, not being forced to defend ourselves from these constant attacks. We are here to protest.

I want to see mutual aid, which there is a lot of already in our communities. You see a lot of it in crowd funders and things like that, but we need to be forming these communities. For example, ACT UP [AIDS Coalition to Unleash Power] used to give each other jobs. One in three employers won't employ a trans person in the UK, so we need to be helping each other.

That's a good way of putting it, because it does feel like you're hitting a wall, so just shifting the narrative is so important. Your activism doesn't have to be yelling at TERFs on Twitter, because all that's going to do is upset you.

CC: It's pointless! I don't want to sound like an old man that complains about social media, because I'm not. I always think that these tools can be used well or they can be used badly.

They're neutral. But when you have no other outlet for anger, it saps the energy for actual change. With actual activism and direct action, suddenly you control the narrative.

For example, let's say you do a sit-in about trans healthcare. The media is not going to report that nicely, because they hate us, but they are going to have to report it at some stage. What they're reporting on is your narrative. They might be reporting it badly, but they're still reporting the narrative. We're giving the narrative, they're pushing against it, and that is the stronger position to be in.

What are you grateful for right now?

CC: I'm grateful that I am where I am. I live with my partner, who's also a trans man. This is the first relationship I've had with another trans man, which is nice because we have a shared understanding that I could never really have with cis guys. Which is fine, but it's really nice to have that shared understanding and to have those shared goals. He's an activist as well. We want the same things and feel the same things.

I'm lucky that I've had people in my life that throughout lockdown have been there to take care of a poor struggling artist *laughs* because we haven't had any work for two years. We've actually been living with my boyfriend's parents, and they're wonderful. They give us the entire upstairs of the house; they don't bother us. I mean, obviously we talk to them, but they understand that we're adults and want our own lives. I'm very grateful that I've got people like that in my life.

I'm grateful my choir is starting again. I am so grateful to be a writer and to have had that creativity. I talk to so many trans men friends, and I'm sure it's the same for trans women as well, about how we are suffering from the after-effects of childhood trauma, and it's not recognized. And I've seen how that trauma has affected so many of us and has made things like interpersonal relationships difficult in many different ways, and, for me, having that from a young age always meant that I had something that I could escape to and go into, and that then became my life, my world. I don't know what I'd be doing without it.

Rico Jacob Chace

Rico Jacob Chace (he/him) is a speaker on intersectionality and non-binary equality. He is a very vocal activist, fighting avidly for the rights of LGBTQIA+ people and black people. Rico started his career as a diversity consultant following on from launching his radio show 'Against Racism' in the aftermath of the Black Lives Matter (BLM) movement. After reporting live at the BLM protests and speaking in the award-winning *Pride & Protest* documentary, he was appointed as a director at TransActual UK. On healthcare, he has also spoken on NHS King's Cross Hospital panels and to North-East A&E doctors on LGBTQIA+ healthcare and a similar subject at the Mayor of London's round-table think tanks.[1]

So you're one of the board members for TransActual UK, an organization

1   'Rico Jacob Chace's Biography.' Chartwell Speakers. Accessed on 13/01/2022 at www.chartwellspeakers.com/speaker/rico-chace.

founded in 2017 to advocate for trans people and educate others about our lives and the issues we face. Obviously, you do offer education for cis people hoping to learn about some of our experiences, but I've noticed that a lot of the work you do is focused on getting facts and support to those of us in the community. Why is that important to you?

RJC: TransActual UK was formed in 2017 after a rise in transphobia, but a lot of the work that we've done kicked off during the pandemic in 2020. I was brought on as a director during the pandemic. We advocate for informed, empowered members of the trans and non-binary community, and we have three main pillars that we focus on. Those pillars were decided by the community itself. They wanted us to focus on healthcare, legislative reform and media relations.

In the healthcare segment of the organization, we effectively did a gap analysis, which means we looked at what other organizations like Gendered Intelligence, Stonewall and Mermaids were doing, and we worked out where we could pool our resources and volunteer expertise from the directors and also from our volunteers to improve things on a wider scale. We realized that a lot of trans and non-binary people do have a significantly large amount of anxiety when they first have those conversations with their GPs, so we created a training session that was offered to organizations as well as individuals that basically went through the legal rights. What does the Equality Act say is discrimination? Are you covered by it, and what can GPs offer you without having to go through the GIC? Most people don't even know, because we weren't really given any training. So that's one side of it – training our own community to have those informed conversations. Some of our volunteers also helped us create a crib sheet for GPs with no background in trans healthcare to make the conversations more equal on both sides.

When it comes to media relations, I do public speaking to raise awareness, and I work as a diversity consultant. One of our directors runs Trans Media Watch, effectively just keeping an eye on the media, developing relationships with publishing houses and reporters. Sometimes, they don't even realize something they've written is incredibly biased, so we suggest ways to make the discussion more balanced.

In terms of legal reform, we do a lot of work with MPs. My colleagues and I responded to government consultations – for example, we did one for the Women and Equalities Select Committee. I deal mostly in public speaking; I did a speech outside Parliament recently. I've done some work with the Department of Transport. It's just really grown from there.

What were you not seeing in the trans charities and organizations that already existed?

RJC: Well, the thing about charitable bodies is that once they focus on one thing, they tend to just have to focus on that. If you're getting funding to do one thing, you're almost obligated to do that. Plus, there is so much work to be done! It's incredible how much work needs to be done, because this country is not aware of the history of trans and non-binary people. They aren't aware that they are responsible for raising the trans and non-binary community. They weren't aware that there are non-binary medical barriers, or there are indigenous identities like two-spirit, for example.

The same way that they've erased the rights of women, erased the rights of people of colour, they've erased the rights of the queer community, so we're all fighting against the same beast. There's been incredibly hard work done by organizations that I've just mentioned – Gendered Intelligence, Stonewall – but we realize that when it comes to something that is trans-led, there aren't many spokespeople or people who are just happy to be in the room and actually point out what needs to be done. So that's the reason TransActual is different, in that sense. But we do work incredibly closely with those organizations. If there is a political decision that needs to be made, whether we're going to be protesting or working with the MPs, we come together and ask what is the best way strategically for our organizations to work as a collective. So it's not really an 'either or' situation; I see some of the legal letters and documents written by people at Mermaids and they work incredibly hard. I'm in meeting rooms with absolute giants – they're so impressive. It's difficult to distinguish our charity from the rest because there is a lot of great work being done by others, Jay Stewart from Gendered Intelligence to name one. I would say we've made an effort to be nationally focused, adult focused and both trans led and run thanks to our 100 volunteers.

On your website, it talks about the founding as a result of increasing hostility against us and our community. I know a lot of us felt and continue to feel a bit helpless as everything seems to be piling up against us; how do you continue to use that anger/fear constructively, rather than let it build up inside you?

RJC: I'm very, very careful of my emotional energy, the emotional bandwidth. You only have a certain amount of emotional band-width every single day, so, for example, if I help a friend through a troubled time, I'm using some of my emotional bandwidth, so therefore I'll make sure to focus on myself for the rest of the day. You have to be careful of your own energy. I purposely stay off Twitter because if I post a tweet, it implies that I care about everyone's opinion. I really don't! I'm here to have conver-sations with established bodies or organizations, as a diversity consultant; I'm not here to argue with someone anywhere else in the world. That's not what I do, or why I'm here. I tend to stay on specific social media platforms for that reason. I would say that it's very rare that I give other people the opportunity to control my emotions. I'm quite careful about where I go and who I speak to.

But I would say TransActual UK, we do have volunteers – we are volunteer-led. No one is on a payroll, myself included. We are just doing it because we think that by pulling together we can make a difference. None of us would have anticipated how quickly we've grown in the last year, but we have volunteers from all over the country. That's one of the few benefits of the pandemic; we can have a meeting and we can invite anyone in the country who wants to help out, including allies. It's a passion project, and I do think that does help me put my energy in place.

That makes a lot of sense! I hate using Twitter because it does just make me unhappy, and I think that is a really interesting point about just knowing where to put your energy. Obviously, I imagine there are a lot of things that you deal with in TransActual that would make you angry, because there's a reason that we need to push for change – there are things that are wrong. But it's specifically using it to make change, rather than just getting angry at TERFs on Twitter, which probably makes it feel a little bit less all-consuming.

RJC: Yeah, I mean I've never, ever had a conversation with a TERF. I'm a bit curious about how they managed to come to their conclusions *laughs* but I don't put it in my schedule because, as I said, I've got other things I need to be doing, a lot of things I need to be focusing on. There are conversations with people who don't quite understand, or they're just allies in waiting, so having constructive conversations with them is a lot more useful than those on the complete other end of the political spectrum.

And I think we're realizing the value of those conversations; I get people who tell me they've got a trans cousin or a trans sibling. The younger generation is coming through, and what corporations will realize and politicians would realize is that even if the older generations aren't quite as understanding – which I take with a pinch of salt because their views and our society has been shaped by things like Section 28 and colonialism as a whole – things are changing. The younger generations do expect gender diversity to be understood by their colleagues, and your client base is also going to be gender-diverse. Things are changing, and we change with it.

*Yeah, absolutely. I started a new job, and I try to go into places stealth and feel out a little bit before coming out to people. On my induction, one of the cis women introduced herself with her pronouns and I was absolutely shocked. *laughs**

RJC: It's beautiful!

It really is, and I've got this circle of trans friends and allies, and I think that maybe I'm just the one who had these fears and preconceptions.

RJC: Yeah, that's the thing. Because you see so much hate online, it's easy to forget that people are actually trying to change and are trying their best. I'm always pleasantly surprised, because my job is to look at hate crime statistics and go into offices and tell people about hate crime statistics. *laughs* But I guess I'm blessed to be in the position where people come to me already wanting to learn, and it's just a case of giving them information, so I guess that spurs me on and gives me more positivity.

During your speech at the Trans Rights Protest this year [6 August 2021], you were very open and honest about some of the experiences you've had in the workplace and elsewhere. I find it particularly difficult to be honest – to myself and others – about some of the hardships I've faced. How did you get to that place of acceptance, and do you think the intersection of your gender made it more difficult?

RJC: In a way, by telling people my story, I'm empowering myself because I didn't feel empowered at that moment. I didn't know my rights, I didn't know about the Equality Act. I was just like, 'Oh, maybe it will stop.' But people aren't going to change their opinions overnight. I think by relaying that, I have a story that gives people a wake-up call. I hope by them realizing what can happen, the impact of their ignorance, that maybe they'll realize that even if they don't necessarily understand trans and non-binary people, they should hold their tongue because everyone goes to work, everyone goes on the train to do something. You're there to work or you're there to travel. You're not there to hear the hostilities. I hope that even if I don't create more allies, at least I educate people on the importance of boundaries and also to recognize the bravery of someone who's going against the way society currently is shaped.

If someone is openly transitioning or mid-transitioning, and being stealth may not be possible, that is an incredibly brave thing to do. So why would you see that bravery and decide to destroy it? It's an incredibly malicious thing to do and I don't think anyone should wish it on anyone. I think people don't realize that by doing that, you are creating severe anxiety, severe depression, and I don't think people understand where that goes. So by telling people this is where it goes, can go, I hope that people would think twice.

I think it is a story that takes people aback, and I do think it makes people stop and think. Is taking control of that narrative something that empowers you?

RJC: Yes, because when I was in that position, mental health wasn't really talked about in my social circle – so no one knew what on earth was going on. I didn't know what was going on. I thought I was going insane because no one talked about depression or anxiety. I was just, 'Why do I have these random heart palpitations? Why are my hands sweating, why are my hands shaking?' I'd be having a conversation with someone and my hands would be shaking. If mental health was openly discussed, I would have realized, 'OK, I need to quit.' There would have been no other option. I didn't realize that it was either my career or my ability to be functioning. If I knew that decision, I wouldn't have thought twice about it. But at the time, I assumed it was just an adjustment process, or I was going to be anxious for a little while, but that's not the way your body works, and no one tells you about that. If you break your arm, it heals. If you break your brain, it also needs to heal.

I also tell that story because I think a lot of people in the community obviously have mental health issues, because of things like abandonment or just the hostile climate that we currently live in. I'm basically saying that I came from hell and back again, and therefore you can, too. It's not impossible. A lot of people don't think that they can recover. I didn't think I'd recover, I really didn't, and that's why, to a certain extent, I did find some solitude at the bottom of the bottle – a lot of us do. We're recovering from our families or a toxic work environment; we have to pretend to be straight. We're just not really processing. There aren't enough healing spaces.

On the TransActual website, there is a specific section dedicated to outlining the importance of amplifying the voices of black trans people and ensuring our activism is more than performative. Was that always something you wanted to platform, in your own work and the work of the organization?

RJC: Intersectionality is so important because you support the person who's being hit the most. The life expectancy of a black trans person in the US is 35, you know; we're literally fighting for our lives. We have to try to have a top-down approach, so as well as helping people find new job opportunities or making employers change their hiring practices, we also have to make sure politicians understand what's happening on the ground. If there isn't a mechanism that relays those stories, then we're not using our resources and our activism effectively. One of the beautiful things about our organization is that if any of us encounter a particular story about domestic abuse, for example, then we can ask if the person is comfortable with us using this quote in one of our submissions. That way, the lawyers who are making these decisions will actually understand what it's like. It's important not just to speak on behalf of people, but to let them speak on behalf of themselves.

So intersectionality is one of the most important aspects when you're engaging in effective activism?

RJC: Yeah, 100%. We're doing a survey right now, and as part of the survey, I said we need to have POC stories represented and elevated. So we had the highest number of POC applicants for a trans and non-binary survey and that happened this year. So we asked a lot of trans and non-binary organizations to advertise it on their page so we can keep pushing the numbers up. We need to tell their stories, and if we get the statistics, we can. We're going to distribute the survey to organizations when they're putting in their submission for funding, so they actually have the statistics to back their arguments.

Basically, it works like this. If you're just saying to a funder that we think people of colour receive more hate, it's less convincing than if you say, '80% of them have received homophobic discrimination and it's disproportionately higher than their white colleagues.' It's a lot clearer that this is an issue that needs and deserves attention. It adds clout to the application processes, and that's really important.

But yeah, the intersectionality front. So, when it comes to

disability laws, trans people who have autism or are disabled often don't actually mention it during their gender dysphoria diagnosis, because people are worried they're going to be questioned if they are of sound mind. That's intersectionality. I have heard some cases of people who have been in wheelchairs or require carers, and the carers actively refused to take them to their appointments. Or if, for example, you are a trans elderly person, can you be confident that you're being properly looked after in a care home? Is your care home going to still give you your shots? There are a lot of instances where your rights could potentially be violated.

But on the POC and trans/non-binary front, our rich history of gender and sexuality fluidity has effectively been erased by colonialism. Anything that wasn't part of that was seen as barbaric, and effectively removed. So we don't know our history, or history has been erased and rewritten by the victors, and we have been written as workers and substandard. We're known as slaves. We weren't slaves; we were enslaved. It's different. So someone who comes out as queer or trans/non-binary in this community is not understood. We do receive, unfortunately, large amounts of homelessness, homophobia, obviously anxiety, depression, abandonment issues. All this does happen, and it has a knock-on impact. Some of the laws prohibiting homosexuality in India were only introduced under colonialism. Our history has been erased, so it's just about revealing and promoting our own stories.

Is that why you focus a lot in the organization on delivering these training sessions?

RJC: I think people just like to say that they're LGBT-friendly.

But then when you go into the actual organization, just look at the management board or even the advisory panel. Who are your trustees? Having one member of the community is not diversity; that's tokenism. And being the only person of colour, or the only person of a particular demographic, it's incredibly difficult. In order to change perceptions of the entire organization on your lonesome, you end up having more arguments than actual progression because people don't understand what you're saying. After a while, it does take its toll. It is exhausting having to educate people on things that you do see as bordering on obvious.

That's another example of directing your energy somewhere, right? If you are the only person in the room, that's what you're spending your energy on. You end up talking to a brick wall essentially, but if you are focusing on giving people those leadership skills, focusing on how to get people's feet through the door, it relieves some of the burden on those standing alone.

RJC: Exactly.

There's a real focus in your work on community and mutual support. Do you think that's one of the core tenets of your masculinity?

RJC: I would say it's a difficult question. I think when I first realized I was trans, I had to look tough. You can see on my Instagram. *laughs* You make this tough guy face in all your pictures. I think it's because your facial structure isn't necessarily as masculine as you want it to be, and you're not on testosterone, so you do anything you can do to promote that really intense manly man persona. Even if that isn't really who you are.

When you begin to pass more, then you end up entering the world of the cis-het man and you start realizing that your height actually matters. *laughs* And I'm quite a bubbly person. I'm quite happy dancing during occasions you could dance, and I was raised being entirely comfortable crying – sad crying and happy crying. And that was OK; I was never told to toughen up.

But then if I was dating, I would end up with women implying that I needed to toughen up because their version of masculinity had an element of toxic-ness to it; it was toxic masculinity. So when they saw me, I wasn't what they expected. You're presented with a decision: whether you have to try to assume this woman's perception of masculinity, or whether you want to change the game and you want to remain yourself and you want to have the confidence in the conviction that someone would still find you attractive and endearing as you currently are.

I have to say, I chose incorrectly. I'd become the problem, and I have seen a lot of newly out trans friends make that mistake. But the older generation, we've come and learned that we have the opportunity to change the game and to be respectful.

Having said that, especially as a Black man, the whole womanizing aspect seems to be perpetuated in the media. My dad raised me well; my dad's a bit of a gentleman so I was sort of raised with those ideals. Until my current girlfriend, I've never really encountered someone who thought that that was normal. *laughs* I always felt as if women thought I was overcompensating, or I was too attentive, or I was too caring, and that seemed quite alien to them.

I find that in lesbian relationships or person-to-person relationships, it's quite common to be nurturing and attentive. But I felt as I entered heterosexual relationships, the traditional roles were projected onto the dynamic. That means that, because you're masculine presenting, somehow you're not supposed to ask your partner how their day was, or you're not supposed to want to hear about their feelings. But I was raised to ask about people's feelings.

And if they're cis, they've probably never encountered trans bodies, and then you're kind of worried if you're being fetishized, or whether you're the new toy. You know that stereotype: let me bring a black guy home to annoy Daddy; the new version of that is bringing home a trans man. *laughs*

I don't find myself dating cis people very often for exactly that reason! It's kind of like I'm a shiny new toy, and I don't like that.

RJC: Just something I can tell the girls when I'm having brunch!

I do think it's interesting the ways your partners' perception of you changed when you began to present different. When I was younger, my concept of masculinity was just 'strong man, never feels anything'. In my experience of knowing cis and trans men now as an adult, that's bullshit, obviously. But there is this kind of perception of masculinity as the pinnacle of strength, but strength apparently just means that you don't cry ever.

RJC: I know what you mean. If I did get emotional before, it wouldn't matter that much. Now, it feels like drawing too much attention to myself because I'm a bloke crying. I did experience it when I was female presenting and I was in same-sex relationships – if I was walking along, cis men would try to hit on the person I was with because they knew I wasn't big enough to do anything about it. Now, because I look like a cis guy, no one really bothers me. I thought that was quite interesting.

That shift in dynamic is so interesting!

RJC: If I'm walking along the street and I look a bit lost, another guy would come up to me and ask if I'm all right. If I was a woman, it wouldn't be the same; it would become almost immediately dangerous, or raising some red flags. Some men actually have conversations with me now – it's quite refreshing.

What is something you'd wish you'd known when you first realized you were trans?

RJC: I think it was the fear. I was absolutely terrified. I thought that my family wouldn't speak to me again, I thought I would lose my family. I thought that I wasn't worthy of love. I was scared of so many things. I don't think people realize how much trans people are willing to put on the line when they do transition. Unfortunately, you put yourself in the situation where you write off a lot of stuff just for your own sanity. And then there are so many moments of trans euphoria when you realize that, actually, everything that I wanted, I can still achieve. I'm a bit of a family man, you know; I've always been quite caring of people. I've still kept all of that. It just transfers over, but I'm just perceived as a sort of family, daddy guy. *laughs* It's the same thing. I'm the same person. So, yeah, I mean, I wish that I could have seen where I am right now. When I first realized who I was, there was a lot of fear and a lot of pain, and I think I was hiding from myself. I would say I would have told myself not to have so much fear.

I remember I didn't get the chance to come out to my parents; I was outed to them. None of us were ready. They weren't ready, I wasn't ready. It was a terrible situation all around, and my dad told me that I was closing doors on myself.[2] I remember that so vividly, and now, here I am, writing a book about being trans, talking to all these other incredibly successful trans men and transmasculine people who are all doing these amazing things, and if I could have told little 15-year-old me that, I don't think that's what closing doors for yourself looks like.

RJC: In a way, you are closing doors. You're closing doors to TERFs. *laughs* I mean, I'm looking to get into a diversity consultancy 9–5, and I got rejected from an application. I spoke to my girlfriend about it and told her I felt really sad, and I wasn't sure if it's because I've just been recovering so my CV looks really patchy, or if it's because I'm trans. She said to me, 'Do you want to work for transphobes anyway?' *laughs* It's true; she's not wrong. I was like, 'How do you get so smart?' *laughs*

But yeah, it's closing doors, but it's closing the right door and it's opening the right ones.

What are you grateful for right now?

RJC: I meditate. I take a lot of comfort in knowing that even if my family did need some adjustment period, they're OK now, but

---

2   My relationship with my parents is now wonderful!

I needed an adjustment period and my ancestors would have loved and respected me. So when I meditate and I think about the ancestors and the strength and the perseverance that's in my veins – that's love, right there. My ancestors were enslaved, so I always think about how if they could survive, if they could go through that hardship, I already have strength in my veins. I was conditioned for strength. If this next meeting or this next conversation or that speech seems tiresome, it's not – because I'm really built for perseverance. That's one of the beautiful things I'm grateful for – my ancestors.

I'm grateful for my family, my sister, for not necessarily understanding – she may not have understood but she helped me anyway. My girlfriend. My girlfriend is so sweet and she makes sure I drink water. She asks me how my meetings are going. She listens to me.

The LGBT+ community, because we're standing on the shoulders of giants. And every new person that takes that step up to do something for ourselves and our community, we're inspiring that celebration and pride and perseverance for someone else from our own generation. And we don't even realize it! I realized I was trans and I spent a lot of time in the POC community, for instance. I interviewed Lady Phyll for a documentary, and so many amazing people. And it was their strength that raises us.

Afterword

During my A Levels, the sixth form had a common room set away from the main school, so we could socialize without the disturbance of those under the age of 17. It was a tad grimy and basic, with square stools set up along the walls and a near-constant smell of stale microwave noodles and vape smoke. No one especially liked me; I was shy and anxious, new to the school but not to the gossip mill, but I joined a group of acquaintances when my friends were in classes and I had an hour to kill.

They were laughing together when I arrived, and I scrolled Twitter mindlessly, half-listening to their banter. Two of the boys were throwing insults in a game of lighthearted one-up-manship. 'You're going to lose your virginity to an old lady!' one said, grinning broadly. 'Well,' the other shot back, 'you're going to lose your virginity to a transsexual!'

The laughter began, then stopped abruptly. 'Sorry,' he mumbled. There was a collective intake of breath, and I hoped they couldn't see the way my shoulders stiffened beneath my jacket.

With eyes trained on my phone screen, I did the only thing I could think to do. 'It's all right,' I lied.

The room suddenly felt incredibly large, and as they shook off the awkward silence to return to their conversation, I could feel myself sinking into it. A vast, stretching expanse of stained carpet tiles and raised eyebrows. I could see it unfold out of the door and into my future, these people who masked revulsion with politeness, who mistook tolerance for acceptance. My desire – my ability to be desired – a filthy secret. An insult.

I am no longer 17, of course, and although, as I write this, it is not terribly far off temporally, those experiences and interactions might as well be a fantasy. Instead, I sit and knit Halloween decorations as my housemate studies. We drink tea together, and I pick at one of the cookies she made for us all. My mother sends the family group chat pictures of our dog at puppy daycare. I type out conversations with men like me and feel the breeze from the open window. All things considered, my life is immeasurably mundane. And it's so full of love I can hardly believe it.

When I first started writing this book, I didn't really anticipate how it would feel to have it exist. I haven't quite taken Caspar's advice and processed my life on paper, but it has forced me to look back on my experiences in a way that I hadn't thought – or wanted to think – necessary. So much of my past makes me sad, so a natural part of moving forward would surely be to leave it behind without a second thought. Yet here I am, leading you alongside me as I reflect on how much has changed. What was so scary about the concept, I realize, was having to do it alone. Throughout this book, none of it has been alone. Kasper and I bonded over the memory of thick black eyeliner. Leo saw me on my first day post-HRT. We all expressed frustration at the memory of pulling on a plain hoodie and jeans to attend our GIC appointments. We have friends and lovers, and we have each other. Whatever kind of book I set out to write, what I have found at the end is a love letter to someone I thought I wanted to leave behind.

I always knew it would be difficult to write a book about masculinity and what it means, because it is both intensely personal and exceedingly difficult to define. I am a man because I am, and none of my behaviours or characteristics could do anything to change that. So this could never have been a 'how to be a man' self-help guidebook, and each interview only served to illustrate that further. What has been discovered here is instead an exploration of unlearning the idea that men are supposed to be anything, that we are bound by expectation and a set of rules to be followed or broken (putting gender-nonconformity on another, slightly different binary scale is deeply ironic, I know). Although we are all bound by community and find our safety and solace in it, the people within these pages are profoundly different, and the realization has been more revolutionary than I could admit. How can masculinity be toxic, constricting, when there are so many ways to be a masculine person? I started by asking what it actually meant to be a healthy man, and came away knowing, with joyful certainty, that I still have no idea. I spent my teenage years utterly miserable in an attempt to succeed at being a man, winning a game that no one else seemed to need to play. Now I am an adult, and more at peace than I can ever remember feeling in my whole life. Being transgender is one of the best gifts I have been given by the universe (the other is excellent eyebrows), and I am honoured to share the planet with my siblings who will continue to surprise me every single day.

After-Afterword

I am, quite frankly, greatly looking forward to re-reading all of this in the years to come and feeling a deep sense of embarrassment at my view of myself, the world and the confidence I seem to have in my own ability to navigate it. I hope I look back and roll my eyes, laughing as I read passages aloud to whoever will be there to listen. I hope I have the same love for me that I now have for the versions of me that have existed.

I say I hope, but I know I will.

I'll see you soon.

Resources

Books

Lou Sullivan, *Youngman: The Selected Diaries of Lou Sullivan* (Vintage Classics, 2021)

Christine Burns, *Trans Britain: Our Journey from the Shadows* (Unbound, 2019)

Shon Faye, *The Transgender Issue: An Argument for Justice* (Penguin, 2021)

Juno Roche, *Queer Sex: A Trans and Non-Binary Guide to Intimacy, Pleasure and Relationships* (Jessica Kingsley Publishers, 2019)

Juno Roche, *Trans Power: Own Your Gender* (Jessica Kingsley Publishers, 2020)

Caspar J. Baldwin, *Not Just a Tomboy: A Trans Masculine Memoir* (Jessica Kingsley Publishers, 2019)

B. Binaohan, *Decolonizing Trans/Gender 101* (Biyuti Publishing, 2014)

J Mase III, *And Then I Got Fired: One Transqueer's Reflections on Grief, Unemployment & Inappropriate Jokes About Death* (Lulu.com, 2019)

J Mase III and Lady Dane Figueroa Edid, *The Black Trans Prayer Book* (Lulu.com, 2020)

Thomas Page McBee, *Man Alive: A True Story of Violence, Forgiveness and Becoming a Man* (Canongate Books, 2017)

Organizations

TransActual UK – www.transactual.org.uk

Gendered Intelligence – https://genderedintelligence.co.uk

Beyond Reflections (formerly Chrysalis) – https://chrysalisgim.org.uk

FTM London – https://ftmlondon.net

Albert Kennedy Trust – www.akt.org.uk

Trans Media Watch – https://transmediawatch.org

Action for Trans Health – https://actionfortranshealth.org.uk

All About Trans – https://allabouttrans.org.uk

Films and TV shows

The L Word: Generation Q (Showtime, 2019)

Chilling Adventures of Sabrina (Netflix, 2018–2020)

The OA (Netflix, 2019)

The Politician (Netflix, 2019)

Disclosure: Trans Lives on Screen (dir. Sam Feder, 2020)

You Don't Know Dick: Courageous Hearts of Transsexual Men (dir. Candace Schermerhorn & Bestor Cram, 1997)

By Hook or By Crook (dir. Harry Dodge & Silas Howard, 2001)

Passing (dir. J. Mitchel Reed & Lucah Rosenberg-Lee, 2015)

Real Boy (dir. Shaleece Haas, 2016)